making
Out

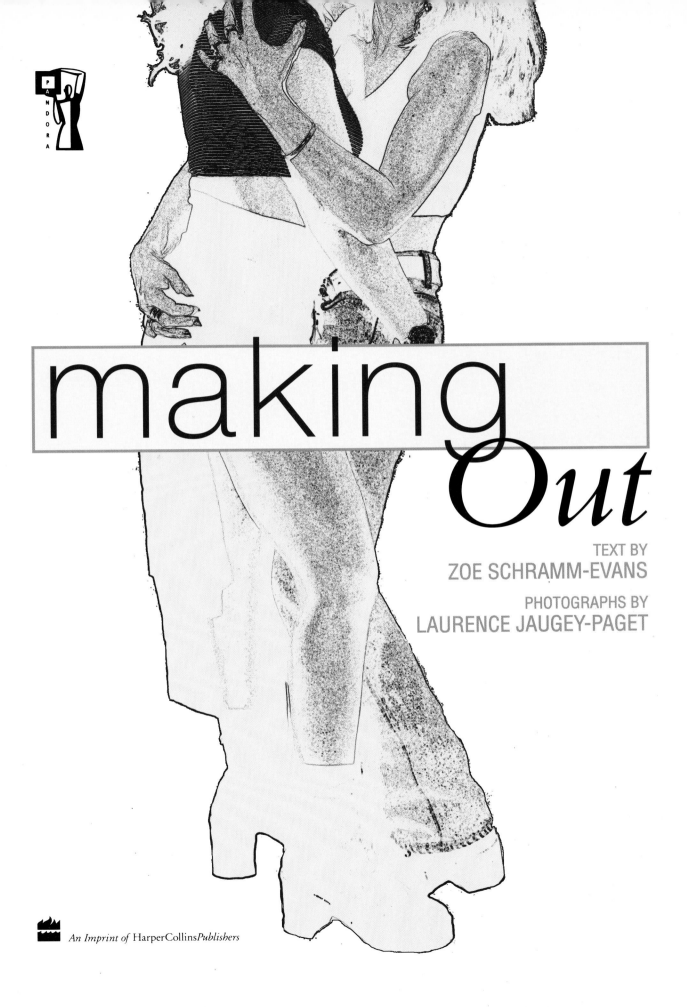

making
Out

TEXT BY
ZOE SCHRAMM-EVANS

PHOTOGRAPHS BY
LAURENCE JAUGEY-PAGET

An Imprint of HarperCollins*Publishers*

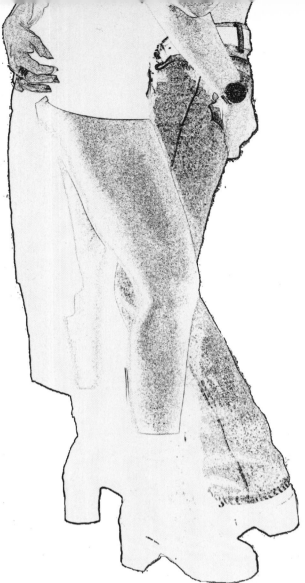

For Deborah Murtagh,
a woman and a friend

Pandora
An Imprint of HarperCollins*Publishers*
77–85 Fulham Palace Road, Hammersmith, London W6 8JB
1160 Battery Street, San Francisco, California 94111-1213

Published by Pandora 1995
1 3 5 7 9 10 8 6 4 2

A catalogue record for this book is available from the British Library

ISBN 0 04 440932 X

Designed and produced by Blackjacks Limited
30 Windsor Road, London W5 5PD

Reproduction by Scanners
Printed in Italy by Newinterlitho Italia SpA

contents

the *Body*

making Out

Anus

The anus is the exit – or entrance – of the rectum, the lowest section of the alimentary canal, and its importance both physically and psychologically has been recognized for many thousands of years.

In some contemporary occult practices, the anus is considered a seat of magic, and in Hindu, Buddhist and Taoist traditions is sited very near the lowest plexus or chakra. Apparently by opening and closing the anal sphincter for several hours, using muscle contraction, it is possible to attain a xenophrenic or altered state of consciousness, merging the conscious and unconscious mind. (If you fail to achieve xenophrenia, you should at least have extraordinarily tight anal muscles.) Continuous internal pressure in the rectum and on the anal sphincters can cause toxicity and headaches and, in extreme cases, hallucination. This led European exorcists, until the 18th century, to use 'clysters' or enemas as a means of expelling the 'demon', often with some success!

The anal canal is about one inch long and opens into the rectum, which is on average about seven inches long; this in turn leads to the colon where faeces is stored before elimination. Like the vagina, the anus is capable of stretching widely. The external anal sphincter is the one which we control voluntarily. The action of the inner sphincter is involuntary, and it is this ring of muscle which needs to be relaxed before penetration of any sort can take place comfortably, particularly if you are a beginner at anal play. Anyone who has attempted penetration before the anus was totally relaxed will vouch for the appalling and overwhelming pain this action can produce. With time and experience it is possible to have control over even the inner sphincter and relax it at will and without stimulation.

The anus is both more and less delicate than the vagina. The vagina is tougher but more prone to infection, and contains the cervix which can become diseased and possibly lead to disease in the uterus. The anus and lining of the rectum are filled with blood vessels which can transmit both body fluids and anything used as a lube directly into the blood stream. The rectum also changes angle, accommodating the spine as it travels upwards towards the sigmoid and transverse colons; you will need to be aware of this if you insert more than a little finger. Anything longer than four inches *needs to be flexible* to fit to the natural curves – hard dildos, or anything else inflexible, can be painful and damaging.

As children it is likely that the only references to the anus we heard were jokes about 'piles' and haemorrhoids. Haemorrhoids, which are varicose veins of the anus, can be extremely painful, and not at all humourous as anyone suffering from them will testify. Anal fissures, small cracks in the anal mucosa, are another common non-transmissible problem which are extremely painful and, like haemorrhoids, can easily become infected or bleed. Both problems can be due to a number of causes, from stress to constipation; both can be problematic for anal sex, as the level of pain or discomfort and the potential bleeding and infection can make anal penetration a turn-off for either or both partners. However, it is now widely known that anal penetration and massage are actually the very best thing for haemorrhoids and fissures. The way the medical profession deals with serious haemorrhoids is through partial 'fisting' under general anaesthetic and giving patients anal stretch devices! So whilst it is not advisable to attempt anal penetration while problems are present (for reasons of discomfort and safer sex) it may be a good idea to consider anal penetration when things have settled down – and not just for pleasure!

Growing up, all of us, whether male or female, learn that the anus is a taboo area. Many lesbians and heterosexuals associate anal pleasure with homosexual men and by extension, with HIV infection and AIDS. In reality, many gay men never have anal sex, and many lesbians and straight couples do it all the time.

Over the last decade it has become increasingly possible to talk about the anus and anal pleasure in a way that simply wasn't possible for people other than gay men. For some women, the idea of fingering, or rimming (putting their mouth or tongue near their partner's anus), or even the thought of buying or using toys specifically for the anus may seem bizarre or even unpleasant, while for others the idea of using such a taboo area to create sexual pleasure, the feeling of being 'dirty', actually heightens excitement. Remember, whatever feels good to you probably is good for you. Women don't all enjoy the same things, but you have a right to your own pleasure as long as it doesn't interfere with anyone else's.

Breasts

For most of history the female breast has been thought of as the essence of womanliness, the source of nourishment and love.

the Body

Some anthropologists believe that the earliest pots and beakers were made in the form of breasts as a reflection of their function as much as their shape. It is thought that the making of pottery in certain places was connected to rituals around the Great Mother and concepts of universal nurture.

Dress since the earliest times has aimed to draw attention to the female breast; the paintings at Knossos depict priestesses covered from head to foot but with breasts exposed and painted. In some African and Pacific cultures, tattooing and scarification of the breasts is practised as an adornment. In Tudor England, women wore bodices which revealed their nipples and thus to a certain extent their age and marital status by revealing the changes that had taken place due to childbirth and breastfeeding; Queen Elizabeth I often wore such bodices at state functions to 'prove' her virgin status.

Old medical texts frequently describe cases of women with more than two breasts (polymastia) or nipples (polythelia). Apparently the statue of the Venus de Milo shows more than two nipples, and Anne Boleyn, the second wife of Hentry VIII, is believed to have been multi-breasted. Both polymastia and polythelia were regarded throughout medieval Europe as a sign of witchhood; the extra nipples were supposed to be the place where the witch suckled her 'familiars'. Any mole, wart, corn or even a larger than usual clitoris could be identified as a 'bigg' – an extra nipple – and as a consequence many women (and some men) were burnt as witches on this evidence alone.

In the late 20th century many women face fear of mastectomy – removal of one or both breasts – as a result of cancer, but the fear of losing a breast is not new. Through history, women's breasts have been excised as a form of disgrace, torture or punishment. For thousands of years women have also agreed to mastectomy, for various reasons: ancient Greek chroniclers refer to the Amazons (from the Greek *a-mastos*, 'without a breast') a female warrior tribe from the Caucasus who were believed to cut off one breast to enable them to draw a bow more effectively. A Russian sect, the Skoptsi, practiced breast mutilation and male castration in order to reduce sin until the beginning of this century.

Because of earliest childhood associations, breasts have enormous symbolic value and are generally regarded as the origin of a wide range of cultural and social behaviours. It is believed that even people who were not breast-fed will have ancestral breast associations which affect sexual attitudes at the deepest levels. In many cultures, the breast is a part of the sexual anatomy of both men and women and an erogenous zone that can give pleasure and even produce orgasm without genital contact. In some cultures however, the breasts are taboo for men to touch during sex, being associated only with childrearing, and therefore 'belonging' to the woman's child.

For many lesbians, their own and their partner's breasts are a central part of their sexual play. As with cunts and clits, breasts and nipples vary in size and shape from woman to woman. Some women may have preferences for what they find attractive, others may not; some women may enjoy firm or even painful stimulation of the breasts or nipples, while others may simply find that intolerable. Our breasts change with our menstrual cycle and what feels good one week may feel terrible the next if the breasts become swollen or tender.

If your sex play starts with a massage session, try pouring oil or lotion over your partner's belly, then moving your hands over her breastbone and round, rather than over, the breasts at first, gradually moving your strokes inwards until she is becoming aroused, then move as lightly or firmly over the nipples and surrounding area as you both enjoy. Some lesbians enjoy being bitten or nipped on the breasts and you may enjoy alternating this with sucking and licking. If you and your partner are both into bondage, you could try tying and strapping the breasts to hold them out and expose them which many women find extremely exciting. You may also like to experiment with nipple clamps or clips.

Some women are able to have orgasms simply by means of breast and nipple stimulation. There is a direct nipple–genital nerve pathway (it is this which causes the uterus to contract during breastfeeding). For other women, having their breasts stroked, kneaded, licked, sucked or bitten is a great form of foreplay, as it gets them 'hot' and causes their cunt to lubricate nicely even before oral or manual contact happens. The feeling of a nipple in the mouth is a very exciting one for many women, and sucking on your partner can be as good as being sucked, particularly when she starts to move with pleasure at what you are doing. If your partner has small breasts it may be possible to suck the whole breast into your mouth – this can be an amazing feeling. If you or your partner have had one or both breasts removed, providing the region is not too sensitive, make it a place for particular attention and loving care, stroking gently and kissing or licking the area; it is possible that nerves in the chest wall will respond to stimuli and give pleasure to both of you. This kind of attention to, rather than avoidance of, a site of loss may help lesbians who have had mastectomies feel good about their new bodies, and better able to enjoy a full sexual life.

Breasts can be very nice simply to lean our head on or cuddle up to when we've had a hard day, before we fall asleep or when we wake up in the morning. They float in the sea and make fun toys; they can be painted to look like eyes or faces or be adorned with jewellery and worshipped.

the Body

Disability & sex

Disability means many different things to each of us, and definitions change constantly. For some women it may mean sight impairment, a wheelchair or crutches, for others a 'hidden' disability like cancer or diabetes.

the Body

Whatever the disability, communication of needs is most important, but this of course is easier said than done. For almost all women, stating our needs is hard, many of us were brought up to put others before ourselves and for disabled women this may feel even more true. If a disabled woman's needs feel so overwhelming that to ask for them to be heard seems like asking for the impossible, then she may stay quiet.

For women and lesbians the world can be difficult enough, but having a body that causes distress physically and emotionally may magnify the problem. There may be a considerable loss of 'self' in being disabled and seeing ourselves as sexual beings is quite likely to be a part of that loss. Whether we want sex or not, we may believe no one could possibly want sex with us and there is great pain associated with this, which many women struggle to hide and which some may convert into anger or resentment. If you have a partner, sharing pain and fear even when it may seem impossible can be a most healing thing. Whether we are with a partner or not, the key to being attractive, whether personally or sexually, must be that we are attractive to ourselves, that we believe ourselves to be lovable.

This can be the hardest thing in the world for healthy people, and a hugely daunting challenge for a disabled person. Our goal can only be to attempt to find understanding and compassion for ourselves and from and for others. Disability comes in many forms, and often those who appear the healthiest are the most needy. Disabled women give as well as receive and can be a source of calm and reassurance. We are all part of the same body, sick and healthy, old and young. We can ignore this fact only at the cost of diminishing ourselves.

the Body

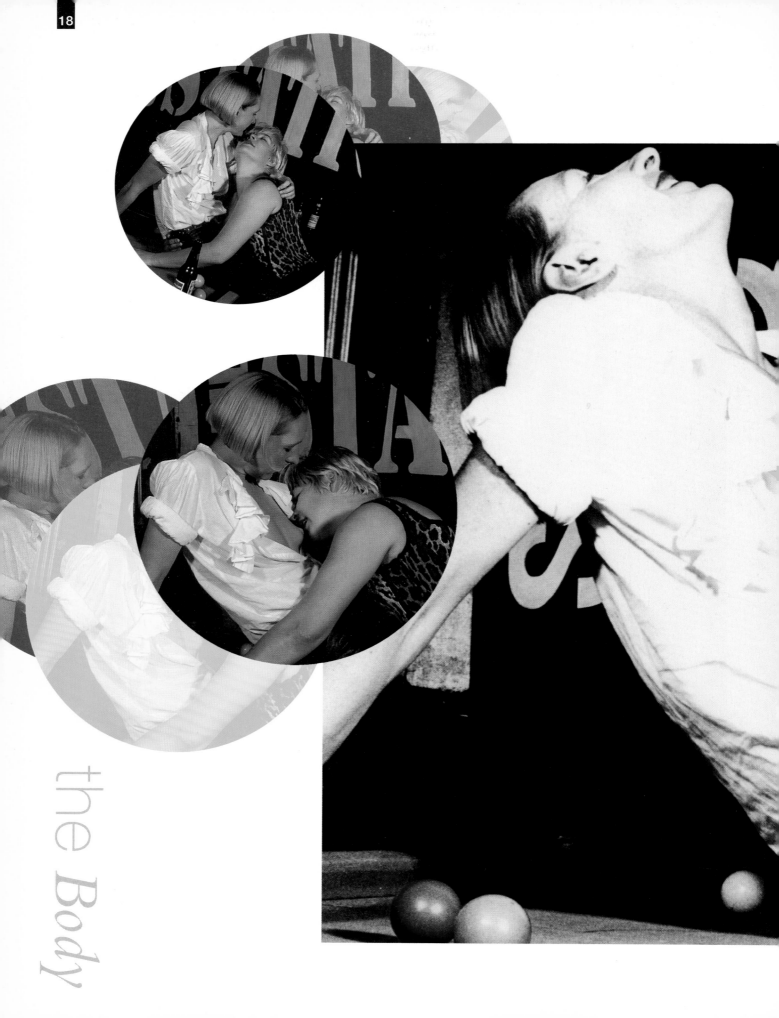

the Body

Drugs & sex

Recreational drugs are the aphrodisiacs of the late 20th century. The rise of the club scene in the 1980s meant that people who might never have considered taking drugs before began to do so on a regular basis.

Lesbians have always been among the most frequent users of nicotine and alcohol (if the meagre research done on the subject is to be believed); but then women who have sex with other women live in a society which deems them unhealthy anyway. There seems to be little indication that lesbians have taken to the new drug scene to the same extent as gay men; this may be partly to do with the fact that women's clubs are thin on the ground so that the opportunities for club use are more limited, and is probably also due to the relatively lower incomes of lesbians.

In terms of sex, there is no doubt that drugs can be a wonderful enhancer. Intimacy and openness to new experiences may be enriched and tactile sensation out of this world; but drugs don't always do these things and can create the reverse, even in habitual takers. Again almost no research has been done specifically on the use of drugs in sex, and most information is anecdotal, much of it inaccurate. One of the few 'sex-drugs' widely tested – because of its alleged links with HIV transmission – is amyl/butyl nitrate *aka* 'poppers'. Poppers can produce brief, intense highs but the are currently considered dangerous as they are believed to lower the immune system. Other drawbacks can be serious headaches – its medical use is as a

vasodilating agent – and it smells of old socks! One of the problems with frequent use of any drug during sex, whether alcohol or ecstasy, is that the sensations experienced can easily become the 'norm' and sex without stimulants and relaxants can seem either boring or inadequate. It's easy to forget what sex *au naturel* feels like, sex and drugs are a powerful combo and the two can become inextricably linked in the mind. This may be fine until you're without one or the other, and then you have a problem. If you actually require drugs to be able to have sex, then it may be that you need much more than any drug is able to offer. Lesbians reportedly have a greater risk of addictions than some other groups, and there may be many reasons for this; fear of homophobia, and perhaps resulting discomfort around sex may be one of them. Only an individual knows the reasons for their own behaviour and even then it may not be clear; but if you feel you may have a problem with drug use, either in connection with sex or for any reason, there are sources of professional help, though unfortunately too few of them are geared towards or understand the needs of chemically-dependent lesbians. Lesbian and gay advice lines will be able to offer practical advice and suggest where to obtain further assistance.

the Body

Menopause

All women experience menopause, the cessation of their menstrual cycle, usually between 45 and 50 years of age. Because sex between women is not based on reproduction, the onset of menopause for lesbians may mean different things than it does for heterosexual women.

However, the physical symptoms will be the same whatever our sexual identity, and these may include thinning of the vaginal and vulval tissue, decrease in lubrication and possible discomfort on penetration. Some women experience hot flushes and psychological side-effects as the ovaries cease to respond to pituitary hormones and oestrogen levels fall. The most difficult thing about the menopause is perhaps having to live with your body in a new way; sex may be the last thing on your mind if the physical or emotional symptoms are severe. Once your body adjusts however, desire will almost certainly return and you may experience a new feeling of freedom around sex. However, you may feel that you no longer want sex at all – and this may be a relief to some women. For women with partners however, it may be a difficult thing to face, for both people; perhaps it means simply changing your sexual repertoire to include new or different ways of being sexual, or it may mean the end of sex altogether. Either way, it's something that will have to be discussed very sensitively.

Making changes at any age is not easy. Very little research has been done on the sexual lifestyles of older lesbians, and this may be because society in general is increasingly youth-orientated and lesbian and gay culture seems particularly so. There are considerable differences in life experience between those women who came out before 1970 and those who did so after. There is much that younger women can learn from those older, and this is particularly true of lesbians who have a great deal to offer and share with each other regardless of age.

the Body

Menstruation

As women our sexual lives revolve to a considerable extent around our bodily functions. Monthly hormonal fluctuations and menstruation, as well as pregnancy, childbirth and menopause, all have a bearing on women's sexual lives to some degree or other.

Some women suffer serious physical and/or psychological difficulties as a result of their menstrual cycle; other women barely notice two or three days of painless bleeding each month. However it affects us as an individual, it may also affect our relationships with our lovers and friends. Some of us may become irritable, weepy and in a few cases downright impossible. Men have standing jokes about their partners being 'on the rag' and there is a whole male mythology about keeping out of the way of flying objects and kitchen knives before and during a woman's 'time of the month'. This type of ignorance and insensitivity has been very disabling for all women and has fed into the perceptions of all sectors of society; gay men are not above making crude observations and even women themselves may see their period as something awkward and distasteful, a constant reminder of feminine 'weakness'. If however, we celebrate our womanliness, our cycle can be seen as a positive thing and enjoyed. Like all women, lesbians will have different attitudes towards menstruation and the fluctuation of their own hormones and that of their partner's. Perhaps you enjoy sex during menstruation and your partner does not; maybe you don't like the taste or sight of someone else's blood and she does. These are all things that have to be dealt with in a lesbian relationship, because it probably happens not once but twice a month. Many women are loving and understanding of hormonal problems their partner may have, but if one woman's cycle is straightforward and the other's is not, this may cause tensions around sex and desire. Feeling loved and cared for when you are low hormonally is very important, and support from your nearest and dearest is vital. If your partner is tearful and tired, try massaging her back or belly, make her special herb teas, brush her hair, offer an orgasm to relieve cramp. If the symptoms are more severe then it really is a medical problem and perhaps the next step is to have hormone level tests or visit an alternative practitioner.

Pregnancy & childbirth

Some lesbian couples have or wish to have children, and in some places at least this is becoming easier to do, both practically and socially.

Getting pregnant may involve sex with a male friend, the use of a friend's sperm or a course of artificial inseminations. Any of these methods can be stressful for a lesbian couple; worries about ovulation, the 'right time' to inseminate and the disappointments when insemination fails can all create emotional difficulties and sex may fade away or be put on the shelf for a while, leaving one or both partners feeling lonely and left out. When one partner becomes pregnant the physical changes that occur, particularly in the first three months, may interfere further

with sexual and emotional life. Throughout pregnancy the desire for sex can fall off completely for some women, and this, added to the physical symptoms of weight gain, can be disturbing for their partner and themselves.

For some lesbian couples the entire pregnancy may be a joy and the baby an addition to an already strong unit. For others, however, it can be a very testing time; the partner who is not pregnant may feel like a spare part. Men often complain of feeling neglected during their partner's pregnancy and childbirth, but they usually have the satisfaction of biological fatherhood; this is not the case for the lesbian partners of pregnant women and mothers, and their own needs for love and attention may not be met for a considerable period of time. It takes a lot of courage, planning and open discussion to surrender an equal role in a relationship, which is effectively what happens, albeit temporarily. A woman may start a pregnancy believing that she will have a loving partner to support her, and then find that the partner may be unable to cope with feelings of superfluousness and perhaps even envy.

If you are single and pregnant or wishing to become pregnant it may be both easier and harder than if you have a partner. Harder because you will have only yourself and friends or family to rely on, but easier perhaps because you will have no one else's intimate needs or wishes to consider. You may not want sex during this time. If you do you may find yourself very popular with some women interested in the novelty of having sex with a pregnant woman. You may want sex with many partners during your pregnancy if you feel that once your baby is born you will be restricted in your activities. Whatever feels right and comfortable is what you should do. Sex is not risky during pregnancy as long as you stick to safer sex and don't overdo it.

Miscarriages can happen to anyone at any time, but fortunately are uncommon in healthy women. If a miscarriage does occur it can affect everyone and it's a time for special sensitivities on the part of lovers and friends alike. The loss is not just the mother's but her partner's also, and the friends and family of bereaved women need to be particularly thoughtful to the couple as a unit at this time.

When a child is born, it's certain that most of your thoughts and actions will revolve around it, whether you are the biological mother or her partner. Sex may not be a priority for some time after the birth and jealousies can arise between couples about time spent with the new child. It's a huge adjustment to go from being a couple to living in a permanent threesome and it can take some getting used to. All kinds of emotional and practical difficulties can push sex right down the list of priorities; but as it's one of the better ways of healing rifts it needs to be discussed and, if appropriate, time put aside for lovemaking and sex play which will bring back some normality into your lives together. If you have a lover who is a part of your life it's important that your children see you as a loving couple who have time for and with each other – no woman is ever just a mother – so that they can learn the skills they will require as adults themselves.

the Body

the Body

Safer sex

One of the more contentious issues around lesbian sexuality over the last decade has been HIV and safer sex. Lesbians have always been in a very invidious social position in relation to HIV and AIDS. At first the popular mythology lumped anyone homosexual into the category of 'carrier'.

the Body

Then, as it became clear that lesbians were the least likely people to contract HIV sexually, they were dismissed and the needs that lesbians did have around HIV, either as people with the virus, as the carers of those with it, or as workers in the AIDS/HIV field, were ignored. Lesbians have been told they suffer from 'HIV envy', that they resent the spotlight falling once again on gay men. Yet they have always been in the very forefront of the struggle against HIV, helping everyone, even those who castigated or ignored them. And of course, lesbians do get HIV just as anyone can. Lesbians can share injecting equipment, can sleep with men – gay or straight – and are as much at risk from unsafe blood supplies as anyone else. It's true that sexually, lesbians who have experienced none of these things are the lowest of all sexually active 'risk groups'; this is not God saying lesbians are wonderful, or even the luck of the draw, it's merely an epidemiological fact.

Most of the leading AIDS organizations have excellent literature and videos on lesbian safer sex, but the guidelines are basically the same for everyone. Ultimately you can't know your partner's previous or even present sexual history – not everyone is able to be honest. Think clearly before you make decisions which may affect you irreversibly, and remember that the virus cannot pass through rubber or latex, so if you have any worries or feel you are uncertain of your partner's health status:

❖ use a dental dam or piece of cling film when having oral sex
❖ use latex gloves for any finger or hand penetration
❖ use only water or silicone based lubricants when using rubber or latex protection
❖ always put condoms on sex toys that are used by more than one person, avoiding ones containing spermicide unless you are having sex with a man
❖ never, ever, share injecting equipment with anyone and when travelling you may consider carrying your own emergency first aid kit with syringes and needles.

If you have any uncertainties about the transmission of HIV or your own personal risk as a lesbian, call one of the AIDS helplines, and if you wish to be advised by a woman ask for this, your needs will be met as far as possible.

HIV has affected the sexual lives of everyone, whether they are conscious of this or not. Our attitudes as a society towards sex, our own bodies and the rest of the world have been changed. As women who love women we can learn to take care of ourselves and our partners while enjoying a vibrant sexual life. Discussing our fears and anxieties can bring us closer together with our partners and with other women in our lives.

the Body

the Body

Sexually transmitted diseases (STDs)

While lesbians are the least likely of all sexually active groups to contract a sexually transmitted disease (STD), they are certainly not immune.

the Body

Not much has been written about the sexual health of lesbians and it is only quite recently that special clinics for lesbian women have appeared in major cities in the West.

This is of course compounded by the fact that many of those in control of the public purse see STDs as a punishment for 'immoral' behaviour and respond by pretending that it doesn't happen. Any 'deviant' – lesbian or gay – sexual health problem is even more likely to be ignored. The sexual health of gay men has been addressed seriously since the mid-1980s though this has largely been as a result of them being perceived as a threat to the 'general public', rather than from any genuine concern for gay men themselves.

Basic hygiene can prevent many simpler infections, and a straightforward matter like wiping from front to back after defecation can prevent infections of the urethra and vagina as a result of contact with faeces. The vulva should be washed with plain water at least once a day and not with soaps or bath products. Avoid douches designed to give 'feminine freshness', these are likely to change the pH balance of your vagina and encourage infections. You should *never* douche if you are pregnant as this may disturb the cervical plug and could cause miscarriage. If your potential sex partner is in poor health, has cold-sores, or simply seems unhygienic or unwashed, don't have sex. If you have sex with male partners, remember that you can contract diseases like gonorrhoea more easily from unprotected sex with a man and you can of course get pregnant! You should be using a condom anyway, to avoid the possible transmission of the HIV virus.

Cervical smear tests and breast examinations need to be part of your regular health care. Many lesbians feel that because they don't have sex with men that they are unlikely to develop cervical cancer; while they may be less likely to do so than sexually active heterosexual women, cervical cancer is *not* restricted to any particular group of women.

Herpes is a sometimes debilitating disease which has several basic forms. Herpes simplex type 1, which causes cold-sores on or around the mouth, is the most common type and is not sexually transmitted, occurring spontaneously as a result of ultraviolet light, exhaustion, during menstruation or in association with other illnesses. Type 2, which is usually sexually transmitted, causes blistering on the genitals which appear about a week after initial infection. The sores appear first as redness, then as tiny clustered pimples which can enlarge and burst forming a single large ulcer. These ulcers can be extremely painful as they are associated with nerves in the region. It is not uncommon to get lower back and leg pain as a result of genital herpes. The lymph glands in the groin region can become swollen and in severe cases walking, urination, defecation and even sitting can be intolerable. These symptoms usually last up to two weeks, then completely disappear and may reappear again during periods of stress, anxiety, menstruation or pregnancy (herpes can be transmitted to the baby across the placenta and during childbirth if sores are present). It is thought that oral sex can transmit type 1 herpes infection to the genitals, though this is uncommon.

Some doctors believe because the virus is robust that it *is* possible to contract the herpes virus from damp towels or toilet seats if the conditions are right, but others would disagree with this idea. There is no cure for herpes, though there are drugs and products which can alleviate the symptoms; these range from very effective anti-viral drugs to locally-applied pure geranium oil or aloe vera gel, both of which are useful analgesics. Any woman with herpes will be a carrier, and although only infectious when the virus is active, it's possible to pass on the virus unknowingly – it can be cultured from the cervix without sores being present – and oral sex with a person with incipient cold sores can result in transmission. It is also possible, though rarer, to autoinfect; for example touching a cold sore or other herpes lesion then touching the genitals – or eyes – can pass the virus from one area of the body to another.

Gonorrhoea is on the increase in the Western world, after years of decline. It is not always easily detectable in women; there may be no outward symptoms and the tests used to detect it are less reliable for women than for men. Gonorrhoea is caused by a bacterium and can attack the vagina, rectum and throat. If you do have symptoms these will appear 2–5 days after infection and might include a vaginal discharge and discomfort on urination, diarrhoea and a feeling of pressure in the rectum and possibly a sore throat. There is some speculation over how the bacterium is transmitted as it is relatively fragile, but in theory at least it can be transmitted on sex toys, fingers and through oral sex, in both directions. The treatment for gonorrhoea is straightforward, being either a single dose or a course of antibiotics, usually penicillin. If it is left untreated the disease can spread and damage the uterus, Fallopian tubes and ovaries, and can cause sterility.

Syphilis is much less prevalent than gonorrhoea, but it too has started to increase again after being virtually wiped out in the West. It is caused by a spirochete bacterium which literally screws its way through the skin at the point of sexual contact. Syphilis is a disease which develops in four stages and first signs of infection may be a chancre or sore at the point of entry which may appear up to three months after infection – this can be on the vulva, the mouth, breasts, anus, rectum or even fingers. The sore, which is infectious, may easily pass unnoticed or be misidentified as it neither bleeds, smells or hurts; many women reach the second stage of the disease without ever knowing they are infected. Secondary syphilis occurs from one to two months after the chancre disappears and a rash or larger lumps may develop, these can appear virtually anywhere on the body and during this stage the spirochetes spread through the body and may cause syphilitic warts – condylomata lata – which ooze an infectious fluid and may become smelly and sore. Some people also develop blisters and scabs on the head and soles of the feet and may have general flu-like symptoms and mucous patches in the mouth or genital area. These symptoms too may pass without treatment but the spirochetes continue to damage internal organs. This is the third, latent stage. In the final, stage of the disease the entire body is often affected; tissue and capillaries are destroyed and without treatment at this

the Body

stage insanity and death can result. Syphilis can be treated at any stage but damage that has already occurred cannot be reversed. As with gonorrhoea, syphilis is treated with antibiotics.

Chlamydia trachomatis is a bacterium which may cause several STDs but most commonly chlamydia, an infection affecting the vagina and possibly the urethra, which in women can result in pelvic inflammatory disease (PID) and salpingitis, an inflammation of the Fallopian tubes which can cause infertility if left untreated. It can cause blindness in new-borns. Chlamydia can be passed through penetrative sex, using your fingers on your partner and then on yourself and through sharing sex toys. It can be treated with a course of usually more than one type of antibiotic, but can be resistant to treatment, so a cure may take some time.

There are other types of serious STDs but they are rarer than gonorrhoea or syphilis; if you think you have any type of STD you should immediately go to a special clinic. Most hospitals have STD clinics attached to them and are used to seeing all sorts of problems and diseases, so don't be put off or embarrassed. If you don't like the way you are treated for any reason, then shop around; in some cities there are clinics specifically for lesbians, so take advantage of them.

Many of the problems affecting the genital area in women are not specifically sexually transmitted. Infections like **candida** or 'thrush', can be related to diet and may cause swelling and soreness of the vulva and vagina with discomfort on urination; it may be entirely symptomless until some form of sexual activity takes place when there may be unusual soreness.

Candida is caused by a yeast and can occur as a result of tiredness, pregnancy, menstruation, and taking antibiotics which affect the pH balance of the vagina. The resulting thick, cottage-cheesy discharge smells rather pleasantly like baking bread! Candida can be treated in various ways, from the traditional – douching with a dilute mix of tea-tree oil, vinegar and/or yoghurt – to the up-to-date – a single dose of oral anti-fungal. The most usual methods are the application of anti-fungal creams and pessaries which can be bought over the counter in most countries. Candida can be sexually transmitted through oral sex – it is possible to get candida in the throat – and through sharing sex toys with an infected partner.

Other infections such as **trichomoniasis** can be transmitted and treated in similar ways to chlamydia and should always be investigated, but it is thought that transmission between women is uncommon. **Genital warts** are also contracted similarly and are treated in a variety of ways, depending on their location. They can be removed with creams or lotions on the vulva, or if they are internal – in the vagina or on the cervix – with minor surgery.

Any STD may cause embarrassment and loss of libido, quite apart from pain and discomfort, and whether it is serious or merely uncomfortable, should never be left untreated. If you think you have got an STD from a partner, it's always a good idea to discuss it with them if that's possible. Some women become angry or upset with their partner if they feel they have been infected with something, but while this is understandable it doesn't help an already awkward situation and after all it is probably most unlikely that the person infected you deliberately or knowingly. Any sexual activity involves risk of some kind, whether emotional or physical and no one, not even lesbians, is immune from that. If you are sexually active with many women, whether you know them or not, it's probably wise to have regular health checks at a friendly clinic.

Vulva

This is perhaps the area of the female body both most and least discussed, enjoyed, despised and fantasized about. The reasons behind these things are manifold, but perhaps the most obvious is that the vulva – the female genitalia – are 'hidden', unlike the male.

The term vulva usually refers to the external female genitals; the Mons Veneris or pubic mound; the labia majora – the outside lips; the labia minora – the inner lips; the clitoris and its hood and the opening to the vagina. It also includes the perineum – the area between the opening to the vagina and the anus. The vagina itself is usually considered as a separate aspect of the genitals from the vulva but in terms of sexual arousal and pleasure they are of course, intimately connected. Words for the vagina and the vulva have been a source of abuse down the centuries, but their first known uses were wonderful. In the Mediterranean world the word originated as *cu* or *cwe* and in Egypt as *ka-t* which referred to the vulva, vagina and mother. Sanskrit words included *yoni* and *cunti* – so no prizes for guessing where 'cunt' originated! *Cunti,* like *ka-t* meant more than just the physical aspects of being a woman, also signifying the female principle. The word 'quim', which is currrently popular with lesbians, originates in the Brythonic or early Welsh *cwm,* meaning cleft or valley.

As we grew up many of us were probably told 'not to touch' ourselves 'down there', and from this many women develop a sense of shame – a sense compounded by the fact that this part of us is often used as a source of insult, particularly by men. Menstruation, also associated with the female genitals, is yet another source of secrecy and shame. Fear of our natural odours causes some women to wash and douche unnecessarily often. Many women don't know that the entrance to the vagina has special glands – Bartholin's glands – which affect natural lubrication and our natural sexual odour, acting as a stimulant to sexual excitement.

Young boys grow up being able to see and compare their own penis with that of other boys, but girls don't have that opportunity and many women have never actually looked at their own vulva or vagina, perhaps because that would mean actively examining 'that part'. Even lesbians may not have a great idea of what is 'down there' until they become sexually active and start appreciating other women's genitals. Then we may wonder if our own are OK. Are they the right size, shape, colour? There is of course, no 'right' anything. We don't really look much like medical diagrams and even the 'gynae-cological' porn on the top shelf shows us that everyone is different. Some women's inner lips extend beyond the outer ones, some are tucked away. A clitoris can be the size of a pea or the size of the top joint of a finger, clit size and cunt size will vary, just as breasts vary in size from woman to woman. The length and width of each woman's vagina will also vary and this may simply be her natural shape, or may alter as the result of having children. The walls of the vagina are thick, ridged and muscular and during sexual arousal 'sweat' lubricating juices. During sex, the walls dilate and the cervix may rise, the entire genital area becomes engorged as blood floods into the vessels surrounding the vagina, vulva and clitoris. After orgasm the swelling dissipates fairly rapidly, if there is no orgasm then it will drain away more slowly, possibly causing aching.

There have been many debates over the years about the female orgasm, mostly foolish arguments about clitoral, vaginal or G-spot types. What has been realized is that the internal structure of our sex organs is much more highly developed and extensive than previously thought. For example, though the visible part of the clitoris may seem relatively small, it is now known that the clitoral shaft extends in a wishbone shape, upwards to the Mons Veneris – the pubic mound – and downwards to end either side of the opening to the vagina. So that tiny – or not so tiny – bud is actually much, much bigger than it appears, just the tip of an iceberg!

The G-spot, another debated area of our bodies, is situated internally between the front wall of the vagina and the urethra – the tube which passes urine from the body. The G-spot is also called the urethral sponge, because it's just that, a layer of dense spongy tissue wrapped around the urethra which can be felt through the vaginal wall. An unaroused vagina is roughly four inches deep and the G-spot is usually located about one and a half inches in. Like the clit, the G-spot swells during arousal and for many women it can be a source of excitement similar to the clit, producing orgasms and in some women, ejaculation. Some women never find their G-spot; some find stimulating it pleasurable, others merely irritating as it can create symptoms of needing to urinate. There are curve-ended vibrators on the market which are

the Body

specially designed to 'hit the spot'. As the G-spot isn't easy to find for yourself – unless you have an unusually short body or extra long arms! – the best way to find your own is maybe to ask your partner to explore for you; some women find that kneeling on all fours or lying face down is the best position for this.

The most 'hidden' and least discussed part of a woman's body in terms of sexual arousal is probably the cervix, the neck of the womb. Rather than being simply the place that babies emerge from, it's now believed to be a further source of sexual arousal, being sensitive to pressure and belonging to the whole pleasure network. The cervix, it has recently been shown, even has the ability to move involuntarily during orgasm. If you want to see what your cervix looks like then you'll need a speculum – an instrument used for internal examinations – a light and a mirror. The speculum can be locked into position, holding the walls of your vagina wide open. Positioning the light and the mirror between your thighs you should be able to see your cervix easily. You could try this with your partner; describing her cervix and the walls of her cunt. Tell her how beautiful she looks inside!

The more we know and understand our genitals – the more we're likely to appreciate their beauty and complexity and feel comfortable with ourselves and our partners. And that can only lead to more fun and more exploration and pleasure – for everyone!

sexual
Imagination

making Out

Aphrodisiacs

The word aphrodisiac derives from the name of the Greek goddess of love, Aphrodite, whom the Romans called Venus. Women and men have pursued the perfect sexual and emotional stimulant for many thousands of years.

Although many substances have been promoted as having aphrodisiac properties, no 'sexual stimulant' has ever been proved scientifically to have a measurable physical effect. It is possible that substances eaten or drunk in the belief that they will cause overpowering desire may have a psychological and hence physiological effect through suggestion.

Among the substances believed to enhance sexual feeling are various foods, perfumes, spices, herbs, medicines and recreational drugs. Only the last of these can be conclusively shown to increase sexual desire and – depending on the type of drug used – this occurs almost exclusively as a result of loss of inhibition rather than from any direct stimulant effect.

The best known and most easily accessible aphrodisiacs are foods like oysters, raw meat and fish – whose aphrodisiac reputations are probably related to the texture and the sensation of raw flesh in the mouth. Potions, philtres and tonics from roots which have a resemblance to the human form, such as mandrake, fennel and ginseng, have long been popular – ginseng is still taken all over the world as a libido-tonic. But not all aphrodisiacs are as innocent in their acquisition and action as, for example, honey or licorice. The rhinoceros is all but extinct in certain areas as a result of poaching by those who produce powdered rhino horn as an aphrodisiac.

One of the most famous of all aphrodisiacs is the notorious Spanish Fly, also known as cantharides, a powder made from crushed beetles native to France and Spain. The powder has been hailed as an aphrodisiac for hundreds of years as it produces an overwhelming itching sensation when taken internally; it is a powerful genito-urinary irritant in both women and men. The beetles contain a chemical capable of blistering skin if locally applied and is potentially fatally poisonous. The Marquis De Sade was accused of poisoning prostitutes by giving them cantharides. These days, the products labelled 'Spanish Fly' which can be bought in sex shops are extremely unlikely to be the real thing!

Aphrodisiacs have been great money spinners down the centuries, and feature alongside non-surgical breast-enlargement and cures for male balding on the list of 'great cons through history'! Having said that, it may be that eating or drinking something that you know is *supposed* to make you feel rampant, even though you know that's nonsense, is still quite a turn-on. Eating or drinking an aphrodisiac is a statement about wanting to feel sexual – and if you want to then you probably will!

Autoeroticism

Coined by a 19th-century sexologist to mean any activity done alone which gives sexual pleasure, autoeroticism is thought by many to mean simply masturbation, but in fact includes a whole range of sexual behaviours, many of which we consider part of our usual sexual repertoire –

touching and feeling our own body, getting gratification from looking at parts of ourselves.

Having sexual dreams, becoming excited or having an orgasm during sleep, is also a form of autoeroticism. Autoerotic activity is evident in small infants, and as attitudes change, adult autoeroticism is now considered by many to be a healthy way of appreciating oneself and relieving stress; but attitudes change slowly, and for some people any form of autoeroticism is still frowned on. Such disapproval probably originates in the historical notion that women had no rights to their own body, that sexual activity was only to be provided by men.

Many women who don't have a lover can sometimes feel unwanted, unattractive, not sexual; we are conditioned into seeing sex as something that happens with an 'other'. Sometimes we have problems with our sexual expression, having orgasms or not, feeling comfortable about saying what we like or want. Often we look for a lover to solve these problems for us, perhaps because we feel that there is something 'not quite right' about sexual pleasure that we provide for ourselves. It's true of course that feedback from another person can heighten sexual enjoyment enormously, but many women find that they can be both more adventurous and more self-expressive when pleasuring themselves than with even the most well-loved partner. It's possible to be totally abandoned, to grunt and groan in a way we may, even unconsciously, suppress with another person. When we pleasure ourselves, what goes into or comes out of our body is entirely within our control, we can touch, pull, contort and adore every part of ourself without any consideration of what another person may be thinking or feeling. For many women, conditioned as we are to always think of others, it can be a very freeing experience. One of the benefits of all this wonderful self-centredness is that rather than making us less interested in sex with others, research shows that women who masturbate frequently have better sexual responses with partners than women who don't.

Some lesbians who have a partner and still enjoy sex on their own may feel 'guilty' about indulging themselves; their partner may feel inadequate or left out. But everyone has different needs for space and for sexual enjoyment, and ultimately we all have the right to our own body and its functions, independent of others.

One of the more unusual forms of autoeroticism is autocunnilingus – licking or sucking your own vulva – which sadly only a contortionist could manage. Inflicting pain on yourself for sexual arousal is called autosadism/masochism and can include: automutilation and autoflagellation – cutting and beating yourself; and autoerotic asphyxia (an arousal technique used most often – but not

solely – by men) which involves cutting off the air supply to increase sexual excitement while wanking. This can be a lethal activity – in the United States alone up to 1,000 people die this way every year. Which brings us to autoassasinatophilia – the staging or fantasizing of your own death for sexual excitement; and autonecrophilia, getting off on imagining yourself as a corpse. Each to their own!

Perhaps the most comprehensive form of auto-anything is automonosexualism, a term coined by yet another *fin de siècle* sexologist to describe people – actually the word was designed to apply to men – who are so utterly self-centred and narcissistic that they can only get off on themselves and have no sexual interest in others at all!

sexual Imagination

Fetishism

The term fetish, which now has primarily sexual connotations, originally referred to a talisman believed by the wearer to convey special powers or protection of some kind. An amulet, locket or bag of worry dolls, if they are thought to have some power beyond themselves, are all fetishes.

In the same way a true sexual fetish is an inanimate object, a shoe, handkerchief, piece of hair or fur, which the fetishist has imbued with sexual symbolism and which she or he – usually he – uses to achieve sexual excitement and orgasm. Sexual fetishism implies that sexual gratification can only be achieved through the use of the fetish. For this reason the early sexologists classified it as a disorder.

Many women use objects to enhance sexual pleasure – whether it's rubber sheets, leather knickers, or a feather boa – but such activities are not true fetishism, but simply a part of general sexual play and fun. While fetishism is most often used during masturbation, it can be fun if you bring your partner into it too. Problems may arise if she dislikes or disapproves of your choice of fetish – a snake, or a dead rabbit skin for example! – but the important thing with involving someone else in this type of fantasy play is to ensure they know that they are the true object of your desire, not the leather harness, rubber knickers, Levis, or whatever. If you feel you have trouble enjoying sexual activities with a partner without your fetish(es), or need someone to be or dress a certain way before they are able to arouse you sexually, it might be an idea to take a long look at the focus of your desires.

These days, the concept of fetishism has become much broader; where fetishism originally implied a highly personal, chosen object on which the user fixated sexually, now it has come to mean something much more public and culturally constructed. We have 'fetish' clubs in the 1990s, places where lesbians can dress up in particular kinds of clothing, maybe leather, rubber, denim or silk and lace. Very often, these styles are part of a broad fashion spectrum, rather than a specific means of individual sexual arousal. The word 'fetishism' has been appropriated by the fashion designers – as it was earlier appropriated by analysts creating a psychosexual jargon. Fetishism has also become closely associated with sado-masochism (SM). Fetishism and SM are distinct sexual behaviours which have been lumped together – mostly by the media and fashion industries – and are currently in danger of being lost to the lesbian imagination in a sea of commercialism.

Our fantasies are our own, we don't need other people to sell them back to us to make them real!

sexual Imagination

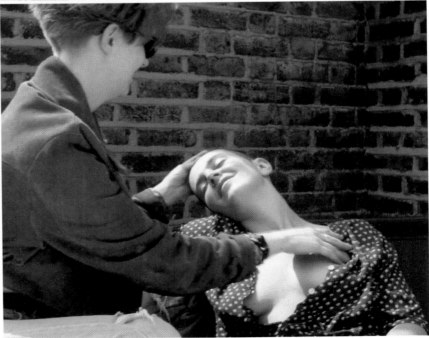

Love & sex

Sex, as we all know, can come in many guises. But perhaps the one single thing that makes sex truly wonderful is loving the person you're making love with.

Loving a woman is not at all the same as 'being in love' with her. 'Being in love' is about desire, lust, possibly even obsession.

While all this can certainly enhance sex, love in its true sense, a unique identification, a being 'one', is undoubtedly the hottest recipe for sex it's possible to have!

Many of us never experience this feeling of real 'love', or do so only in flashes. Most of us are too busy trying to get what we want from our partner, trying to control her, trying to 'give' things that may not even be appro-

priate. Sex is one of the very few places in our ordered and controlled lives where we can truly be the animals that we are beneath the leather and Levis and business suits. Many women fear sex, which is not surprising because it's a fearful thing to let go, to admit to being part animal. To introduce powerful emotions into an already difficult equation seems like asking for more trouble and yet as women it seems natural to do so, few of us find it easy to fuck without feeling *something*, even if it's dislike.

Just as sex can be a putting aside of the barriers of the outer, physical self for a few minutes, hours or days, so love – real love – is about a putting aside of ego, needs, desires, and even hopes, and creating an openness to life and to another human being. When the physical and emotional come together on that sort of level, no drug yet created can beat the feeling of absolute totality, because it represents not only the sexual interaction but the whole of life and love.

These are undoubtedly romantic notions, and as such many might say they are impractical in 'real' life. That may well be true. But if we can't at least aspire to them then what is love and what is sex? If sex is about more than babies – and for the majority of gay people it is about more, or other, than that – is it simply physical pleasure? If it *is* only pleasure, where are its limits? Well, we are certainly limited by the capacities and dimensions of our bodies and are likely to be so for the foreseeable future. Are we limited by our imagination? It would seem we are – research indicates that there are far fewer 'perversions' and 'deviations' around today than 2000 years ago! Our

sexual imagination has not even kept pace with technology and is less interesting by far than that of our ancestors who didn't even know what a toilet seat was! Human sexual imagination is limited to a very few basic ingredients – pure lust, power games and/or commitment – and that's about it.

The least realized tool at our disposal is love in its profounder sense. The combination of *real* love and *real* sex equals passion, as opposed to desire which is usually stereotyped even if we are unaware of this. Passion is not a popular construct these days, it implies too much loss of self and control, but – and this is the whole point – isn't that what it's really about? Passion is not something that we can experience with just anyone, it requires judgement and wisdom to choose a partner with whom we can *truly* 'let go'. But it seems that in our need not to be alone, not to be without sex at almost any cost, we inevitably sacrifice passion in favour of something much less.

To have an orgasm in your heart when your lover touches your lips with her fingers, now wouldn't that be something?

Sexual Imagination

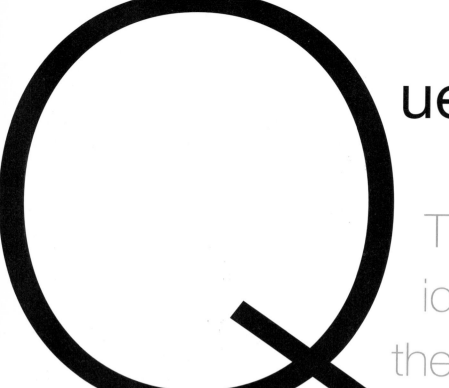

Queer

The new identity for the end of the century appears to be 'queer'.

Lesbian, gay, bisexual – we're told by the gay and straight media alike – are concepts which are beginning to wear thin. Whether we choose to go along with what we're told and embrace the new queer world, or whether we prefer to ignore it and hang on to our identities is entirely up to us, though there's no doubt that pressures from within a 'community' are harder to ignore than those from without.

Until recently 'queer' was used as a term of abuse against gay men, like 'pansy' or 'fag'. In the 1990s it has been 'reclaimed' by gay men and lesbians and is now most frequently used as an umbrella term for 'alternative', and implies anyone or anything not 'straight'.

Heterosexual people can therefore be queer too, provided their lifestyles or sexual practice are not 'straight'. So, for example, a hetero-sexual couple seriously into sub/dom, SM or threesomes could be very queer indeed! Queer also embraces concepts of 'genderfucking': 'transgender identities' and transexuality, and 'gender insubordination', all of which can be serious and useful attempts to address gender stereotyping. Or possibly be a reflection of an individual's inability or refusal to accept his or her self in the context of society. Or may be little more than a new way of describing the more hackneyed notion – 'role reversal'. Girls can be boys and *vice versa*, but most of us knew that anyway; that it needs to be stated is perhaps the most interesting thing about it. Maybe one of the most positive things about queer is that *anyone* can be, even straight people. But then again, who *is* straight?

The question to be asked by all of us is not "How do I identify sexually?" but "Am I honest with myself about my sexual desires and the acknowledgement of my own gender?" If the answer to this is "Yes", then the question of identity is already resolved.

Queer claims to be breaking down barriers, which can only be a good thing – though doubtless many would disagree. Doing so within the existing parameters of sexual identity inevitably means that queer exposes itself to a repetition of the problems inherent in the 'communities' and identities from which it stems, and so becomes a cultural tautology. When we next strap on a dildo and tell our lover to suck it, maybe we should question the feelings and reasons. Does our sexual imagination only go round in circles, is there room for a lateral sexuality? When we next look in the mirror perhaps the question to pose is "Do I *need* yet another 'identity'".

Taboo

Taboo, like fetish is a word appropriated by psychoanalysts from so-called primitive culture. Taboo is a Polynesian word for an object, person, gesture or act which is prohibited by social or religious custom. All societies have taboos of one sort or another, and there has always been an ambiguity around the concept of taboo.

Freudian psychology described a taboo as something that was at once sacred or consecrated, but at the same time, unnatural, dangerous, forbidden or unclean.

It has been suggested that the separation in ancient times of menstruating women from the rest of a group, and the rules surrounding menstruation itself, were the foundation of all taboos, rituals and initiation rites. From earliest times, women would spend the period of their menstruation in specially designated places, often allowing their blood to fertilize the earth. During this time young women would be taught the 'mysteries' of sex, fertility rituals, contraception, the uses of herbal poisons and medicines and ritual magic. The secrecy surrounding these exclusively female activities, and the much more evident procreative function of women, is thought to have aroused envy in men and caused them to create their own initiation rituals and mysteries. Over the many thousands of years since that time, women have themselves become taboo in many cultures and menstruation has become something shameful and dirty, to be avoided by men at all costs. Having sex with, or even touching, a menstruating woman is strictly taboo in many cultures.

Perhaps as a result of the taboos around menstruation, the monthly cycle is regarded by many women as a 'curse', something which we may hate and despise, rather than celebrate in the way our ancestors did.

The reverse side of this taboo is the belief, still held by some, that menstrual blood is a powerful aphrodisiac and in some societies – 18th-century eastern Europe and Germany in particular – it was part of love potions and rituals. The connection between the phases of the moon and menstruation caused menstrual blood to be regarded as the elixir rubeus – the 'red elixir' – a vital aspect of sex-magic rituals and alchemy which was at its most powerful during the full moon.

Besides menstruation, some of the most common taboos in almost all societies are those around murder, certain types of food, incest, interracial sex, virginity, illegitimacy and homosexuality. Which taboos operate in a particular society are reflected in the use of 'dirty words'. In 1976, a North American university conducted a survey of the 'tabooness rating of 28 dirty words' in descending order of offensiveness. They were motherfucker, cocksucker, fuck, pussy, cunt, prick, cock, bastard, son of a bitch, asshole, suck, nigger, tits, whore, goddam, shit, bitch, piss, slut, queer, bullshit, ass, spic, blow, jesus christ, damn, hell and pig.

Nearly twenty years later, some of these words seem perfectly polite! One or two of them, the lesbian and gay community have retrieved for their own use, such as 'cunt', 'pussy', 'cock' and 'queer'. The words indicate that the society which used these taboo words was primarily white Anglo-Saxon, male-dominated, homophobic and 'Christian'.

It also dislikes pigs! Sex acts and associated parts of the body predominate, which says a lot about how we, as a society, see sex and our genitals.

Ironically even lesbians who are completely comfortable with their sexuality, their bodies and their activities can be caught in the 'taboo trap' of culture; only now it's lesbian culture which has created those taboos and this can affect not only our real life, but our fantasy life too. Many lesbians feel guilty if they fantasize about having sex with anyone other than their partner, having lots of sex with lots of women, having sex with men, being paid for sex, getting raped – either by women or men – having under-age sex, liking sex too much. The list is endless. Some women may fear that a fantasy is a prelude to reality – that they really want to be abused or raped. There is no indication of a correlation between fantasies and reality on this level. There is however, a correlation between the 'tabooness' of an object or fantasy and the erotic symbolism with which we endow it – in other words the more forbidden a thing, the more loaded with sexual glamour it

becomes. Our minds seem to be naturally attuned to the pull between the 'pure' and the 'impure' and if we choose, we can use taboos to fuel our erotic dreams and activities, rather than destroy them.

Feelings of guilt around sex with men may arise from a feeling of 'letting the side down', the fear of ostracism and loss of community. However, as lesbians explore their heterosexual feelings, taboos around this sort of activity will doubtless change, until hopefully all fear of difference is resolved and the potential fluidity of desire is acknowledged by all sexualities.

Taboos are part of our human history and how we regard them and whether we acknowledge them will depend very much on our cultural and personal histories. Which we choose to keep and which to give back is up to us, we may actively enjoy or use certain taboos or restrictions. If however, we feel that our lives are restricted in any way that feels uncomfortable because of taboos – either social, cultural or personal ones – then maybe we should consider why they are important to us. History was then – this is now!

Virtual reality sex

Virtual reality sex is sex for the 21st century, so we're told – or rather masturbation for the 21st century.

Anyone who has watched Jane Fonda in *Barbarella*, seen Woody Allen's *Sleeper*, or Stephen King's *Lawnmower Man* should have a fair idea of what VR sex is all about.

The technology we have today was designed by the American military for use in flight simulators and targeting systems. At present, the hopes and expectations surrounding virtual reality technology have gone way beyond the 'reality' and are still only 'virtual'. What scientists are racing to produce is a means of creating all the sensations, smells and feelings of actual sex with a person of your choosing by electronic simulation in 3-D.

Currently, if we have US$45,000 plus to spare, we can wear a VR helmet or visor which incorporates a video screen and data-gloves and sit in a chair which tilts and moves with our body and gives hot and cold sensations. If you have a computer you can link the screen to your VR visor and join in VR games with other users via the modem. As yet there is nothing available which can truly simulate sex as there is no genital data equipment on the market. What *aficionados* of this type of experience are waiting for is the 'teledildonic suit' which would connect all the visor and audio links to the erogenous zones and could be used solo – for looking at pre-recorded programs – or for networking with others similarly linked. Cybersex, as VR sex is also called, is currently available in audio versions and it's now possible to buy

3-D audio compact discs with titles like 'Cyborgasm: Erotica in 3D Sound'.

How do all these things affect lesbians – if at all? At present, the market is run almost exclusively for and by men, although the producer of 'Cyborgasm' and editor of *Future Sex* magazine is a woman. Ultimately VR/cybersex is about doing it alone, it's the polar opposite of 'real' interaction, which for many lesbians is what sex is all about. For some people the idea that sex is becoming increasingly separated from any kind of personal interaction is scary. Sex is important to women because it remains one of the few very intimate and fundamental aspects of our already over-technologized lives, if that too becomes a prey to technology, why go out of the house? Because it is largely created by and for men, VR sex is already a big part of the porn industry of the United States and becoming so in Britain and Australia; the lines between VR and porn are already blurred and will probably get more so. Already such things as 'The Virtual Photoshoot' are available, where the 'photographer' can order real-life 'glamour' models around on screen, then print out the work or make it into a video. In a decade or two men will be able to experience and explore the things forbidden to them in 'real' life, such as rape, torture, murder, paedophilia, without fear of consequences – the victims are only electrons after all. Before long you may be able to copy pictures of anyone you fancy fucking onto the bodies of models, giving them whatever size and shape of breasts, legs or genitals that you want; then have sex with her, or make her have sex with someone or something else.

What, if anything, should be done about such technology is hard to say, it's still too early to predict what the personal and social results might be. The serious addiction problems that some adolescents and adults experience with arcade and home computer technology will probably get worse if such experiences are physical as well as psychological. It is fairly inevitable that the ability to suit-up and enter a 'virtual' world more pleasant and co-operative than the real one will have profound effects on our understanding of the world we inhabit. At present, men are thought to be far more interested than women in VR sex, which may say a lot about gender interaction! Some women would argue that cybersex is not about sex at all, but about an ultimate control. On the more positive front, cybersex is the ultimate safer sex, the sort of sex you dress, rather than undress for! If any of this stuff really happens in the future, sex in the 21st century will be undoubtedly be colder, cleaner, more bizarre, but probably much less truly imaginative.

What we already have are computer/ modem Bulletin Boards, which include CompuServe's 'CB' facility, putting gay men and lesbians – with 'handles' (names), like 'Detroit Dom' or 'London Girl' – in touch with each other all over the world. Then there's the phone sex or 'fantasy service' industry which is believed to be already affecting the 'real' sex industry in some countries. Thousands of women and men work in 'virtual' prostitution and many more work creating stories to be read out live or recorded, which include fantasy stories for lesbians. There are also the phone dating services, which offer recorded messages from women wanting to meet other women for sex.

However the future of sex looks, it's unlikely that anything yet thought of will surpass the experience of real sex at its best; but at its worst ... who knows, maybe cybersex will have something to offer?

Voyeurism & exhibitionism

Though these activities imply the opposite of each other, they share the feature of involving other people, often strangers, in sex at a distance.

Sexual Imagination

Voyeurism and exhibitionism can be done alone; with a partner or a friend; or in a group situation – at a club or party for example. You can watch and be watched in almost any imaginable situation.

Many of us, if given the opportunity, might watch an attractive woman, or possibly a man, undressing, dressing, bathing, masturbating, or making love. Not many of us might admit to doing, or wishing to do such a thing; we might think of it as 'spying' and we would hate to think of anyone watching us in private moments. Some women, however do get a kick from taking their clothes off in front of windows at night with the light on, or walking naked around the house during the day with the blinds up or curtains open. Some of us enjoy wanking where we might be observed; in public places such as the underground, the bus, the back of a cab – when someone noticing might just guess what's going on, but never be absolutely sure. There may be no designated urban cruising areas for lesbians, but there are women who've been taking strolls involving solo sexual pleasure around parks and public places for years – maybe seen, but never caught!

For most women who enjoy these sorts of activities, they are little more than an occasional, even accidental means of excitement or interest – something to be taken advantage of if the opportunity arises – a sort of distant 'casual' sex. For some people however, they may be the main form of sexual arousal and in these instances voyeurism and exhibitionism would be considered a sexual disorder. Exhibitionism in men, usually in the form of 'flashing' is often considered a form of power demonstration, or a means to achieve the extra thrill required to achieve an erection or orgasm. In both women and men, the need to exhibit themselves either sexually or socially can become compulsive, an extreme form of 'showing off'!

Most art forms involve some sort of voyeurism, the artist as observer, watching, either through painting, photographing or writing about what she sees. Every time we watch a film we become voyeurs and every time we dance in a club or a party we are exhibiting ourselves. Watching and being watched are part of being alive, doing so in a sexual context can enrich our fantasies and our relationships – it all depends on how.

sex
Gear

making Out

Anal toys

Like dildos, anal toys have a long history, and come in many shapes and sizes. Though it's gay men who appear to have explored the erogenous possibilities of the anus to their fullest, this part of the body is a pleasure zone for women too, and we are now beginning to reclaim it in our sex play.

This is reflected in the types of toys that are being sold in lesbian sex shops.

While it's fine to use a straightforward vaginal dildo for anal sex, there are good reasons for obtaining an item specifically designed for the anus; one reason being that, unlike the vagina, the anus is not a 'dead end' and it is possible – because the rectal muscles are able to draw up into the body as well as push out – that the object inserted will 'get lost' if it is small enough. It is not uncommon for objects as varied as carrots and the lids of hair-gel containers to get stuck in the transverse colon and require a general anaesthetic or even surgery to remove! Hence the numerous embarrassing stories repeated by doctors and nurses about patients' (usually male!) midnight trips to hospital casualty departments!

Most toys designed for insertion into the anus and rectum come into the category of butt and ass plugs, which are usually a diamond or 'christmas-tree' shape and are designed to be 'worn' rather than used for thrusting. Most anal plugs have a narrow 'neck' around which the external anal muscles close – this prevents it falling out – and a flat base which stops the plug disappearing into the rectum. Though the basic shape may be a diamond, the surfaces of plugs vary from smooth to ridged or rippled and the material used is similar to that used for dildos – rubber, vinyl, silicone, steel or wood. With harder materials such as steel, care needs to be taken

during use to avoid hitting the interior aspect of the spine and the coccyx . When inserting, all anal toys should be angled slightly forward, away from the spine.

Some women prefer the smooth-sided plugs that leave them feeling expanded and 'open' anally, while others prefer the sensation of the anal muscle opening and closing as the ridges or undulations of the plug move past it. There are anal toys made specifically for those who enjoy the open/close sensation: certain specialist manufacturers make toys of steel balls of the same or differing sizes set up to an inch apart on a T-bar, corkscrew-style handle.

Perhaps the least known type of anal toy are 'beads', which is literally a string of up to six beads in rubber or plastic strung on washable cord with a ring at the end for removal. This particular toy was a favourite with far eastern courtesans many hundreds of years ago. The beads can be the size of a pearl or a tennis ball and are inserted one at a time and then pulled out either singly or all at once, gently or quickly as a means of intensifying orgasm or simply feeling good.

There are a number of anal vibrators on the market. These stimulate the lining of the rectum, sending waves of sensation throughout the area, and are also very helpful in relaxing the anal sphincter and allowing penetration to take place. If the vibrator is large or of dense material such as rubber, the vibrations of a battery-operated motor may be rather weak, a harder material such as plastic may give a more intense vibration (but again care must be taken when inserting these less flexible models). Some steel plugs come with hollow tubing intended for electrical wiring, but unless you're an experienced SM *aficionado* or an electrician, these may be best left alone!

As with dildos, butt plugs can be worn with a harness to keep them in place, but unlike dildos they are internal rather than external. A harness can be worn round the thighs, or you can simply string rope through the base-ring that many plugs carry and tie it as you like. One of the reasons for bothering with a harness would be if you intended to wear the plug under clothing, while at a party, going shopping or just tidying the bedroom! They can be particularly enjoyable to wear when travelling. Many people cite a motorbike ride along bumpy roads as their favourite journey, but a bus or train might do just as well!

Dildos

For many women the word dildo conjures up the image 'fake penis', but the dildo is undoubtedly in a class of its own.

A dildo is any item designed to penetrate the vagina or anus. Dildos have a long and honourable history – featuring in paintings and text dating back many years BC and are part of the art form of many cultures.

Dildos come in many and varied shapes and sizes and are available – if you know where to look – in pretty well any material, including plastic, wood, leather, bone, silicone, steel and rubber jelly. Shapes vary from 'realistic' penis types – some of these are moulded from the size-X genitals of famous porn stars! – to the body of a woman, a fisted hand, or a streamlined dolphin. Some women make their own dildos with loving care, while others spend hours gazing at heaps of carrots, cucumbers or zucchini. Dildos can perform almost as many functions as the imagination of their user can come up with, but they can be bought for specific functions. Dildos specifically for anal use are often referred to as butt plugs and can differ in size and shape from vaginal types (see Anal toys).

Strap-on dildos are currently very popular with some women, as they allow total body contact from all angles during penetration. They are sometimes worn in public as fashion item, gender statement, or just for a laugh.

When used with a male partner, strap-ons undoubtedly bring an entirely new dimension to fucking. Most strap-on dildos are single-ended, the part fitting the wearer's body usually worn against the pubic mound and clitoris, giving stimulation through rubbing and pressure. Double-ended dildos allow simultaneous penetration and can create a unique joint vaginal experience. Most strap-ons are attached around the waist and between the buttocks, but they can be made to fit around the thigh, leaving the genital area free. Strap-ons, while extending the range of our activities, aren't always the easiest things to manage and can take a little getting used to – after all, they aren't a feeling part of the body and we only really know what we are doing by watching and listening to our partner's reactions. Used without due care and attention, dildos can damage the cervix and in extreme cases the uterus; if used carelessly in the anus, they can damage the delicate lining of the rectum and even the gut itself.

Among the vast and growing range of dildos available are inflatables, which are controlled by a pump similar to that on a blood pressure gauge. These can be inserted either partly inflated or empty and then pumped up to the desired fullness. They aren't the easiest things to handle, as the lube makes them slippery and they're likely to fly out, but the experience of variable pressure at crucial moments – particularly if someone else is in control of the pump! – can certainly make it worth the effort. Dildos can be bought with suction cups that will fix them to the wall, chair, table, floor or wherever else it will stick, leaving the hands free for other things. Metal dildos, while they require particular care in use, provide an interesting cool, smooth sensation. Leather dildos are usually handcrafted and very expensive, and should always be used with a condom as the stitching is impossible to clean adequately and the leather dyes and fixes can irritate internal membranes.

Remember, dildos used without a condom should not be shared, as they can spread infection from person to person; nor should they be used anally and then vaginally. To prevent infection and cross-infection it is easiest to have a number of condoms to hand and change them as required (see Safer Sex).

Perhaps because of the involuntary movement and dilation of the vagina during sex, many of us enjoy or even demand penetration, and finger-fucking isn't always enough, while fisting may be too much. In such circumstances a dildo can be ideal. Of course, for some women, dildos seem too 'male' and their use too much like heterosexual sex. But there is no reason why a piece of plastic or rubber used to heighten sexual enjoyment either alone or with a partner has to be identified with anything beyond itself – any other interpretation is simply a cultural construct. A woman's cunt is her own. Just enjoy!

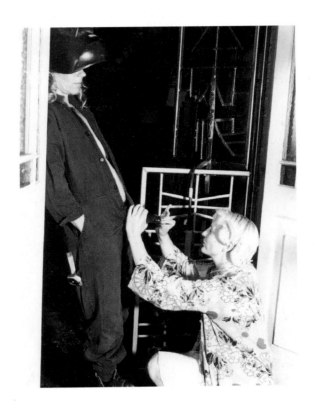

Lubricants (lubes)

Most women lubricate naturally when sexually excited, but the amount of liquid produced will vary from woman to woman, some producing very little and others creating a waterfall. It isn't known for certain how vaginal lubrication occurs, but the fluid is secreted from the walls of the vagina as excitement grows.

The amount of lubrication will also vary dependng on the time in the menstrual cycle. Some women feel that if they aren't wet they aren't excited; while that may be true in some cases, it certainly doesn't always follow. If you have reached the menopause, have had a hysterectomy, have just given birth or are breastfeeding, then you may experience a natural dryness. It is thought that vaginal lubrication is a reponse to oestrogen cycles, not sexual arousal alone.

If you are using sex toys for vaginal penetration you may well want to use a lube to prevent chafing; if you are using anal toys you will almost certainly need one; if you are having sex over an extended period of time you may find that you dry naturally and need something extra. There are lots of different kinds of lube available on the market, long gone are the days of Vaseline and KY as the only options for smoothing the way during sex.

If you want a completely natural lubricant try egg white or certain vegetable oils. Oils or creams intended for moisturizing are not a good idea because they will be absorbed into the vulval tissue too rapidly, and probably contain chemicals which can irritate the delicate membrane of the labia and cause inflammation or lead to infection. Although an old favourite, Vaseline does not wash away easily and can stay in the body for days, and along with other heavy mineral oils can lead to yeast infections. Any oil or oil-based products will destroy rubber, so condoms, dental dams and even your favourite toys will quickly perish and die! It is also possible to irritate the opening to the urethra with some creams and lubes, so do choose carefully. The best available lubes are either water-based or silicone types. Water-based lubicants come in varying forms, some thin and liquid, others thick and dense, it's simply personal preference and trial and error to find which you get on with best. Water-based lubes do have a tendency to dry out after a time, so you may like to have water handy to rejuvenate what you've already applied rather than simply use more. Silicone lubes can be more expensive than water-based types but feel like oil and don't dry out; they do, however, stain fabric in the same way that oil does.

Many specialist lubes come in flavours, and though some of these can be quite pleasant, many taste disgusting and artificial and may remind you more of strawberry or banana shampoo than your partner's natural juices. Much erotic writing has discussed the pleasures of eating from your partners cunt or anus; things like whipped cream, chocolate sauce and jam may be fun and taste good, but they can lead to the same kinds of infections as certain lubes and may be best confined to other parts of the body. Horror stories of people using things like facial scrub and hair conditioner abound, so think before you lube! Whatever kind you choose to use, it should be pleasant for you and your partner.

Sex Gear

SM gear

One of the simplest techniques for starting a sado-masochistic (SM) scene and assuming roles is bondage, or restraint as it's also called. This involves using ropes, chains or straps to tie the women in the role of bottom down – to the bed, the chair or table.

She can also be tied standing or kneeling. Some women like to assert their authority as top in silence, others to let the bottom know who's in charge verbally as well as physically. It's very important that restraints are not too tight as this will reduce circulation which is unpleasant and may distract from what else is going on. Some women prefer to use ropes for bondage and this can be as simple or as intricate as you like. Bondage *aficionados* may spend many hours tying and untying a bottom, taking pleasure in the sophistication of their ropework. Chains and leather strapping may have more textural appeal for some women than rope and these are popular but can be more expensive and less easily obtained. If you are into a light sensous restraint, silk can be very erotic. Simple bondage might include the use of handcuffs and legcuffs – don't lose or forget the keys! – and perhaps a collar and lead, easily found in any pet shop.

Clingfilm is becoming increasingly popular as a bondage tool. It's cheap, available and useful in the kitchen too. It has the advantage of being a quick, simple but very strong method of restraint – a few wraps around your partner's body and she can't move. It can also be used in long and very involved scenes for 'mummification', where each finger and toe, leg and arm is individually and carefully wrapped before the actual bondage process begins. This can take may hours and is only really suitable for women who enjoy total

restriction practices. It can also be a fast way of losing body fluid, as you will sweat copiously!

There is a wide range of highly specialized bondage equipment available these days, including belts, cuffs and ankle restraints which can be quickly hooked up together and released. If you are into suspension – a rather sophisticated form of restraint – then you will need specific equipment to do this safely which may include some form of harness and hoist. For experts only!

What can be safely used by anyone with the space and wall-plastering to take them are simple suspension items like slings. Slings come in many sizes and designs and their purpose is to support the body, legs and arms as the bottom lies – usually on her back – with limbs restrained to the four suspension straps which hold the sling at waist height above the ground. Slings are usually in a basic H shape and might be a whole leather hide, or latticed strips of rubber. The suspension straps need to end in large, heavy-duty metal rings; it's these rings attached to hooks in your wall/scaffold/four-poster bed or whatever, that support the sling. Because it's going to take a person's full weight the sling attachments must be very secure and strong. Slings are popular with people who enjoy enema and shaving play; fisting scenes; extended play with dildos or butt plugs and the use of electrical equipment. Some women use slings for straightforward fucking. The bottom is rendered totally helpless and the rocking motion adds to this by denying her any sense of being grounded as she hangs in mid-air. For the top, a sling gives conveniently-placed access to all parts of her partner's body with the exception of the back. The legs are spread widely and the genitals exposed in a way that can be very exciting for both partners.

One of the simplest but most effective forms of bondage involves restraining the senses. Blindfolding and gagging can render a person more helpless than limb restriction and in a more subtle way. A blindfold can be created from whatever you have to hand, or may be highly crafted from soft leather with silk lining. It's all up to your own taste and imagination. Gags similiarly can be purchased from a range which includes ball-types, designed to keep the mouth open around a plastic or rubber ball, or bit-types which are usually a length of firm rubber or plastic tubing designed to bite down on. If none of these appeal, you can always use a stocking, bandana or anything you think suitable. Some women who are into SM enjoy using clamps or clips on the nipples, vulva or clit, for extra sensation. There are many sorts of custom-made clamps available, some with rubber ends and some with 'crocodile' teeth, for the very serious! You can improvise with clothes pegs, bulldog clips or anything that takes your fancy in a stationer's or ironmonger's.

There are an increasing number of shops specializing in SM gear, some catering particularly for women. If you live away from a major city, most of the larger SM shops sell their products by mail order, so you should still be able to get what you want. If you have a good imagination however, you may notice all kinds of items in all sorts of shops that can be used for SM activities – ropes for restraint, candles for hot wax, clamps and leather straps and whips can be bought cheaply almost anywhere. SM doesn't have to be the extravagant activity that some people like to make it. It's what you put into it at the time that matters. SM on a shoestring is as good as any other sort, and it can be fun looking in the window of an ironmonger's or a saddlery and seeing the items in quite a new way!

Sex Gear

Vibrators

The history of the vibrator is not as long as that of the dildo for technological reasons, but is almost equally honourable. The first steam-powered massager was invented by an American doctor in the mid-19th century, for the treatment of women's 'problems' – i.e. lack of orgasms, then called 'hysteria'!

By the turn of the century there were many different styles of vibrators in use. Up until the 1920s vibrators were advertised as 'health' promoting, as conferring a healthy vitality and a 'glow' to the women who used them – the potential for masturbation was never mentioned of course, but adverts assured purchasers that they would experience thrilling, tingling sensations! While cures for 'women's 'problems' became increasingly psychological rather than physical by the 1920s, the vibrator as a health-restorer remained popular, offering to cure anything from migraine to tuberculosis. When vibrators started appearing in early porn films in the 1920s the source of the marvellous tingling became obvious. As the sexual possibilities of vibrators were exposed, 'decent' publications gradually stopped advertising and writing about them.

One of the main selling-points of a vibrator as a sex tool for women is that the intensity of the vibrations can help anorgasmic women to reach orgasm, either alone or with a partner. It is also recommended as a sexual aid for people with disabilities who may experience reduced sensation in the genital area as the result of injury or illness; powerful vibration may be felt where the touch of a hand or mouth might not. There are types that can be used without hands and this too may be a pleasurable discovery for disabled lesbians. In the United States there are research and manufacturing companies which specialize in adapting and suggesting sexual products for disabled women and men.

Some lesbians get great pleasure from their vibrators and while most are perfectly happy with this, some may feel bad, imagining it's taking something away from their partner if they have one, or that it's unhealthy in some way. Unhealthy to enjoy yourself too much?! It's possible that if you go too strong with a vibrator during sex with a partner that you can get temporarily numb and have to wait until you can feel what she's doing to you, but that's not a big deal surely? Vibrators are something that can be shared – with proper hygiene naturally – and *can* be used not just for genital stimulation but for all-over relaxing body massage too.

If you decide you would like to buy a vibrator, or even try a new design, you might like to think exactly what part of you or your partner's body you intend to stimulate, and then look around at the designs available before making a choice. If you are going to share the toy, take the same hygiene precautions around cleaning or using condoms that you would with a dildo, bearing in mind that the motor can be ruined by water. Never use a mains operated vibrator *anywhere* near water, or you may get a 'buzz' you'll never recover from! Avoid using a vibrator, or any sex toy for that matter, on sore or broken skin, it may make the problem worse and can spread infection to partners or even other parts of your own body – candida for example can be passed from vagina to throat or rectum.

Vibrators come in many different guises – from the clinical-looking 'massager' that can be purchased in the local pharmacy, to a huge rubber dildo-type with battery-operated heart! The types most currently available tend to be battery-operated, which give a less powerful vibration than the plug-into-the-mains sort and may 'die' at crucial moments! The most commonly available vibrator is the cylindrical type which is either a smooth 'rocket' shape, or penis shaped. These come in a variety of materials, from hard plastic to pliable silicone in exotic colours, though colours are commonly pink or black. The hard variety give the best 'buzz', because the vibration of a large or even small, rubber or silicone variety is lost in the material itself and transmits as a rather frustrating tickle! Cylindrical vibrators are probably not the best kind for clit stimulation and are unlikely to produce vaginal orgasm unless you are used to getting off just being penetrated anyway, but they can be great fun if you enjoy anal or vaginal sensation while stimulating your clit

manually or with another vibrator. As with dildos, vibrators probably need to be used with lube for comfortable insertion and use.

Certain types of vibrator designed specifically for clit or vulval stimulation are becoming available in this country. These are known as 'wand' types and are a mains operated variety with a round, soft, rubber head and make a whirring sound. Very few vibrators are soundless and depending on how and where you use one, this may pose problems! Other vibrator styles include a curve-ended design specifically for stimulating the G-spot; types for combined vaginal and anal penetration, some shaped like a thumb and index finger; there are strap-ons which can be worn to stimulate the clit or inserted into the vagina and held in place by a pouch attached like a G-string or dildo harness.

There's a whole world of possibilities out there, take advantage of them – if you, or you and your lover, are about to start a relationship with a vibrator, have a great time together and who knows, the next time you go to a girl's club the atmosphere may be truly buzzing!

Sex Gear

sex

Acts

making Out

Fisting

Fisting or handballing as it is also called, is the term used for inserting the whole hand or fist into the vagina or, sometimes, the anus. While some women consider fisting to be strictly part of SM sex, for others, fisting is a part of general sex play, albeit a rather special part. Of course, fisting is not for everyone.

Although for many women fisting may seem a new and/or gay male practice, it has been around a very long time as an occult discipline throughout the world, used by men and women of all sexualities to achieve heightened states of sexual awareness.

If you experience problems with penetration, have had a hysterectomy, or are post-menopausal and have more fragile vaginal tissue, fisting may be best left out of your sexual repertoire. It is usually not recommended to get involved in something as potentially delicate as fisting if either partner is under the influence of alcohol or other mind/body-altering drugs. However, it is precisely in these states that sexual extremes tend to occur; so great care needs to be taken, as most substances reduce awareness of pain and injury and when sensation returns it may be too late.

Many women who are into fisting report experiencing greatly enhanced orgasms. Although this may be partly physiological – the actual pressure on the walls of the vagina and the cervix is considerable – it is almost certainly psychological and emotional too. The hand is arguably the most sensitive and therefore intimate part of the body, having a sensory capacity even greater than that of the genitals – more nerves run from the hand to the brain than from any other part of the body. Experiencing your hand disappearing into your partner's body, or theirs into you, is unique, and in some people produces profound cathartic experience and an almost mystical feeling of union. For some women, the ultimate sexual experience involves double-fisting – one hand in the vagina, the other in the anus – while with no free hands, the tongue can be used to stimulate the clit. The sensation of being totally filled and stimulated genitally can be utterly explosive, sometimes to the point that orgasm becomes irrelevant. (Sometimes pressure and excitement reach a point where the person being fisted may lose bladder control; if you're into watersports, no problem; if not, be prepared!)

The first rule of all fisting is to remove all jewellery from the hand and wrist. Ensure that nails are filed smoothly down to an absolute minimum – internal tears may not be felt but can still cause infection. Some women prefer to wear latex gloves for fisting, but logically if you don't use a glove to finger your partner there is no reason to wear one for fisting either. For anal fisting it is almost always necessary to douche thoroughly first (enemas can be part of foreplay if done properly as they can be both stimulating and relaxing and some women really get off on the unusual sensations of the warm – never hot or cold – water flowing through their insides); some people even fast beforehand to avoid potentially awkward situations – although if you have a particular interest in scat (playing with shit) then this won't be necessary.

For vaginal fisting, start by stimulating the vagina with the tongue and fingers.

When your partner is sufficiently relaxed, apply a great deal of lube to the whole hand and the vagina. (Some women find that amyl nitrate (poppers) helps relax the whole body and the genital muscles in particular, but this is *not* recommended as unresolved health questions hang over the use of poppers at present. See Drugs and sex.) Begin penetration with one or two fingers; by the time you've worked up to four fingers your palm should be facing upwards. If your partner is well into it at this stage she'll probably be bearing down on your hand. It's important as you press in, to co-ordinate the movement of the knuckles past the outer ring of vaginal muscle with the tucking in of the thumb and curling of the fingers into a fist. All this may seem rather complicated, but with a little practice it becomes a smooth single movement.

Once inside your partner's body the sensation can be quite overwhelming, but there are many things which can heighten both her and your enjoyment. With your free hand you can explore the rest of her body, stroking and relaxing. The inserted hand can be moved in and out as gently or as hard as your partner feels comfortable with. The hand can be twisted back and forth to produce an unusual 'screwing' sensation, or the fingers can be carefully opened to increase the pressure.

Some women prefer the hand inside them to be removed carefully and gently, others find that to have the hand abruptly removed during orgasm heightens sensation. To feel the movement of a woman's vaginal muscles contracting around your hand as she orgasms is a very special sensation. It may take a while for both partners to 'come down' after the action – a time for special closeness.

Group Sex

Group sex has been around as long as sex itself. It's only in the last hundred or so years that sex has come to be considered a private act between two individuals. As an 'art form' the practice of group sex (or orgies) was probably raised to its peak during the Roman Empire.

Some of us may have images in our mind of 1950s films showing dancing girls, human torches and fat old emperors! But the history of group sex goes back even further and is closely related to the practice of occultism or sex magic, the practitioners of which believe that it is possible to harness the bio-energies created during sex – hence the more people, the more energy for making magic. For many lesbians sex with a number of other women and/or men is a popular fantasy. More and more women are starting to explore group sex in reality, either with friends or strangers.

Because many behaviours around sex are still taboo in our culture, it can be extremely exciting and novel to watch other people having sex if you've never seen it before – and most women haven't, except on film. On the other hand you may feel embarrassed or self-conscious; there's no doubt that taking part in group sex is about performing. Physically, group sex can beat other forms of sex hands down – literally! Anyone who says many tongues, hands and cunts are not better than one has never experienced them. However, if it's emotional intimacy that you look for in lovemaking, then group sex is possibly not your thing.

If you are considering having sex in a group which includes your partner, it's probably important to have discussed this very thoroughly beforehand. However prepared you imagine yourself to be, if you have never seen the person you care for most in the world being fucked by someone else, you *will* have feelings to contend with and they may not be the ones you expect. If one of you wants to have sex with other people as a group and the other doesn't want this, then you may also have some talking to do. Similarly, if you are considering a group sex scene with friends with or without a partner, think clearly of the ramifications beforehand. Will you be able to look each other in the eye the following day?

For the single and heartfree lesbian, group sex could be the answer to all sorts of things! You get to meet lots of women and instead of having to wade through them one by one, you get to cut the chat, find out what they're like sexually and whether they have any future potential, all in a single scene! While it's true that lesbians value the emotional aspect of sexual relationships, it's also true that an increasing number of lesbians are looking for sexual encounters with women that are simply that – sexual. Group sex can be an ideal situation for this, as the reduced intimacy can actually create a 'safer' emotional environment and the greater physicality can provide the purely sexual enjoyment that some women want.

If you decide you want an orgy, plan carefully, there's nothing worse than getting into a party and realizing you've run out of 'whatever'! Get in the videos, the music, candles, toys, plastic sheets, ropes, massage oil, booze and whatever else you plan to use to make it all go with a swing! You may find yourself opening a club one day! Who knows?

Sex Acts

Masturbation & orgasm

For most women, masturbation is the first sexual experience they ever have. For many women it's the most fulfilling, in sexual terms, whether they are lesbian or straight.

Despite these realities and despite the cultural and social changes which have made masturbation more 'respectable' over recent years, it is still unlikely to be a topic suitable for the parental dinner table, or perhaps even one's close friends. Masturbation is probably the best learning technique for good sex with a partner, whether you're sexually inexperienced or an old hand. You find out where everything is; how it works; maybe what it looks or tastes like; you can find out what will or won't bring you to orgasm and share this with a partner. Some women rarely or never masturbate, preferring to feel that arousal and/or orgasms are something that other people 'give' them. While this may be OK if you're in a sexual relationship, it's impractical if you're not and even if you have a partner, it does rather hand over the responsibility for 'creating' sexual pleasure to another person – who will, of course, also have the power to withhold that pleasure. Sex surveys have shown that women who masturbate are more likely to be orgasmic than women who don't. However, masturbation can be much more than a means to an end, it can be a wonderful way for getting in touch with your own unique sexual responses, by and for yourself alone.

Why is it that some women can come anywhere, anytime, anyhow, with anyone and others may come rarely or perhaps never? Why do some women lubricate more than others, and some ejaculate on orgasm? Research indicates that all women are capable of orgasm, but this ability can be affected by a number of things: firstly there are psychological factors; in addition, certain prescribed drugs, some recreational drugs, alcohol, spinal injury, illness or pain can all affect our response to sexual stimulation. Clearly we are all different physically and psychologically. While the former can't really be changed, the latter can. If there are parts of your sexual experience which you would like to be different: if you would like to have an orgasm and never have; if you would

like to experience ejaculation – then go for it. You may not get what you want, but you should have some fun trying.

Wanting something *too* much can of course be the very thing that prevents it, so relax as much as possible. Masturbation is ideal for all kinds of experimentation, there's no one to be concerned or embarrassed with. Many 'how-to' books on women's sexuality give tips and techniques for achieving orgasm and while some are unhelpful, there are some very good manuals around suggesting exercises for anorgasmic women; so take advantage of them if orgasm is something you would like which still eludes you.

Orgasm is a muscle spasm which occurs as a response to sexual stimulation; the extensive network of nerves in a woman's genitals are further connected to the breasts, spine and brain amongst others areas. Many women find that the rate and intensity of their orgasms can be controlled by creating deliberate muscle tension in the pelvic floor and upper thigh area as this appears to enable the nerves to be stimulated more quickly and easily. Try tensing your pelvic muscles outwards, as though your legs were being pushed apart and simultaneously closed, while stimulating your clit with your hand or a vibrator; vary the muscle movements until you find what feels the best.

Female ejaculation is still a hotly debated topic even among lesbians. Some people believe that women's ejaculate is simply

urine leaking as the bladder relaxes during orgasm; others think that as the walls of the vagina 'crash' together during the muscle contractions of orgasm, natural lubricant squirts out under pressure.

Some women apparently ejaculate a milky substance through the urethra in the same way that men do, which is similar in composition to male prostatic fluid and quite different to either urine or vaginal juices. This type of ejaculate seems to be related to stimulation of the urethral sponge or G-spot which is thought to produce the secretion. Relatively few women report experiencing ejaculation of this latter type – obviously there's a lot of research still needing to be done on this important biological and cultural topic.

Masturbation is probably the simplest and least problematic of all sexual behaviours, unless we still have hang-ups about it. What it can't give us is interaction with another person and their body and feelings, sounds, smells and touch. Masturbating with or in front of your partner can be a real turn on for both of you, a kind of private show. You can take turns as the voyeur and exhibitionist, or be both at once! This kind of interaction has lots of advantages: your lover can learn without verbal instruction exactly what you like and what gets you hot the fastest or slowest, as you prefer, and of course it's the ultimate in safer sex. You can show your partner things you love to do on your own but may have always been too shy or embarrassed to talk about; slipping your finger into your anus and then sucking it as though it were the most natural thing in the world may convince both you and her that it is!

Masturbation can be a constant friend and support. It's there when we're supposed to be too young to have sex and still there when we're supposed to be too old to want it! It can bring literally years of pleasure. It can be a solo or shared experience. It can relieve migraines, menstrual cramp and frustration. It's our own to do with as we choose.

Oral sex

Oral sex – cunnilingus, going down on, eating out – is probably the most enjoyed and least talked about form of general sexual activity. There are no laws against oral sex in the United Kingdom but in the United States almost half of all states have laws against adults of the same gender engaging in this activity and nine states have laws against married people of the opposite gender enjoying oral sex!

Given that an estimated 50–90 per cent of all sexually active people have oral sex as part of their usual lovemaking, these laws may seem downright weird, but like masturbation, oral sex is a non-procreative activity and it may just be that the killjoys of the world don't like the idea of people coming – literally – up against the bare facts of life.

For some women, oral sex can seem alarming, all of our five senses are brought into immediate contact with our partner's genitals, their smell and taste. For lesbians this means, in some sense, a mirror image, which can be a profound experience psychologically as well as sexually. Some women have anxieties about their own odours or taste and may find the idea of someone going down on them unappealing. However, unless an infection is present, or you haven't washed in days, any smell or taste will be perfectly natural and acceptable to your partner. If you feel uncomfortable in any way, just shower or bathe beforehand, preferably without using soaps or scented products – these will erase your own natural odour and many women find the taste and smell of their partner's cunt very exciting. After all, that is what our natural odours are meant to do, excite us!

There are many ways to enjoy oral sex, and finding the position that is most comfortable for both you and your partner is important. If you are having an extended session of cunnilingus you may find that you have a sore jaw after a while, that you can't breathe, or that your tongue gets tired. There are no awards for endurance, so have a rest, come up for air, relax your face and tongue. Too vigorous licking can damage the frenulum, the cord of membrane under the tongue – this isn't serious but can be painful for a few days until it heals. (One of the ways to avoid problems is to do a lot of cunnilingus and build up your facial muscles!) If your partner is lying on her back, build pillows under her buttocks and raise her up so that you are moving slightly downwards rather than up – this will relieve tension on the neck and relax the tongue. An alternative position is to have your partner straddle your shoulders with her vulva over your face, by wrapping your arms around her thighs you can keep her precisely where you want her to be when she starts wriggling with excitement. A well-known variant of this is the '69' position, where one partner lies on her back and the other kneels or lies in a head-to-tail direction. Like this you can go down – or up – on each other simultaneously. Try imitating each other's actions until you get the feeling that you are actually licking yourself – it can be mind-blowing, particularly if you enjoy coming at the same time (although it can be difficult to concentrate on your partner when you are experiencing bliss!)

Because most oral sex involves being at a distance from your partner – it's possible but not easy to look into someone's eyes when your head is between their legs – it may be important to keep contact, either through the woman being licked, stroking or touching her

partner's head or arms, or holding hands. Many women enjoy being penetrated during oral sex and find that finger-fucking, either vaginally, anally, or both, is an incredible combination with cunnilingus.

One thing that may need to be discussed with your partner is how you both feel about oral sex during menstruation. Some lesbians actively enjoy the taste of menstrual blood and its signification of womanhood, others are simply repulsed by the idea of doing such a thing or having it done. If you want to have oral sex during a period and don't like the taste of blood for yourself or your partner, try inserting a fresh tampon beforehand.

The name usually given to oral stimulation of the anal area is rimming, the dictionary terminology is analingus. While many of us might find the idea of licking, sucking or inserting the tongue into the place that shit comes from abhorrent, as with almost any sexual activity, with adequate hygiene there is no reason why it should be unpleasant or off-putting if it's something you feel you might like to try. The anus is full of nerve endings and it certainly can feel as good to have it stimulated orally as any other part of the body (some people might say better). One thing to be remembered about rimming however is that it's possible to get infectious diseases such as hepatitis or internal para-sites this way, but if your partner is healthy then there is no risk of this happening. As with any form of anal sex, you might want to douche or have an enema before rimming, or ask your partner to do so. Some people argue that it isn't a good idea to lick the anus and then the vagina as this can transmit infections, but if an anus if clean enough to lick then it is unlikely to cause this sort of problem. Because the anus is an area of tension for many people either physically or psychologically, having it touched and licked can be very relaxing for many women, while for others the very fact that it's taboo makes rimming unusually exciting.

Penetration

For many lesbians, penetration whether vaginal, anal, or both, is an extremely important part of sexual life; for others it simply isn't important at all. Unlike other sexual activities between women, for some lesbians penetration implies hetero-sexual sex, penises and men – and for these reasons, penetration may be avoided.

Surely, anything that two women do together can only be inherently lesbian, even if they were consciously to imitate heterosexual activity? These days as women explore their interactions with each other through gender play and, amongst other things, the development of a queer culture which embraces all sexualities (and none), questions of the 'correctness' of a behaviour seem at last to be fading away in favour of pleasure for its own sake and for many women, penetration can be supremely pleasurable.

Of course, preferences around penetration vary hugely, both from woman to woman and for the same woman at different times; it may depend, for example, on your menstrual cycle. Before and during menstruation the cervix drops and the vagina shortens; this can make penetration uncomfortable, and so some women might find anal penetration more pleasurable, or likewise no penetration at all. Fingers are the objects most commonly used for penetration by lesbians, they're always available and incredibly sensitive. But during the history of womankind, anything that can fit has probably been inserted into a cunt at some time or other! Vegetables, dildos, vibrators, hands, feet, golf balls, gearshifts, chocolate eclairs, penises, light bulbs, deodorant bottles, hairbrush handles, candles, snakes, fruit, rolling pins – they've all been there!

Whatever gives you pleasure, either on your own or with a partner, take time out to enjoy something new or different. If you're familiar with dildos, try a vibrator; if you often use one to two fingers, try three or four; use different kinds of lube. Combinations of oral stimulation and penetration can be particularly exciting for some women, while others may find it too distracting or even desensitizing. Many lesbians say that orgasms reached with and without penetration vary in quality and degree. Orgasms from clit stimulation alone tend to be localized and intense, while orgasms during penetration, with or without attention to the clit, are more diffuse and whole-body centred.

For the partner doing the penetrating, the feeling of being inside another person's body can be as exciting as being entered oneself. The warmth and wetness of a partner's cunt, or the tightness of their anus, can be an incredible turn-on and some (very lucky!) women can orgasm simply from pleasuring their partner. The muscular power of the involuntary vaginal and anal contractions which many women experience during orgasm may be surprising to you when you first experience them with your fingers inside your partner, or you may have felt your own while masturbating. Anyone who believes that women can successfully fake an orgasm obviously knows nothing about how women climax!

You or your partner may enjoy the experience of penetration using strap-on dildos or vibrators, and these can add a different dimension to your sex play as they leave your hands free for caressing, massaging, slapping and holding. Some lesbians enjoy oral penetration with dildos as part of gender games and this too can create a new sense of fun – particularly if you try coating the dildo in something nice-tasting, honey, chocolate sauce or you partner's own juices.

Anal penetration is a no-no for many lesbians, but for others it can add a whole new dimension to sex. Some women would argue that two are more fun than one and both at once are best of all! If you're already into anal penetration, try using a vibrator in your partner's cunt and your fingers in her anus, maybe your tongue on her clit too – why not spoil her! Or you could do it all the other way round – vibrator on her clit, fingers in her cunt, while rimming her. The combination of possibilities is only limited by your imagination and your partner's enthusiasm and flexibility! If you're into major stimulation, try dildo-fucking her anus, with a vibrator in her cunt, or vice versa. Always remember that what one person goes mad for, another may loathe, so save your best party-tricks for the woman (or women) who enjoys the same things you do.

If you are new to anal sex, try finding out what you like yourself with some anal masturbation. Using plenty of lube, stroke the anus until it begins to relax then gently insert a finger, it should be comfortable and feel hot and good inside. Move your finger around and if it's all easy and comfortable, try a second or third finger too. (Some women, with practice and some degree of contortion, are able to fist themselves anally, a unique sensation.) Whether you wish to reach this stage of anal practice alone or with a partner, or are perfectly happy with some gentle stroking, just do what feels good and no more. Many women may have been put off anal sex after a bad first experience – try again, slowly and comfortably this time and perhaps you'll change your mind. But if not, then don't fret; there's no inherent virtue in liking or not liking *any* kind of sex act.

Entering a partner's body, whether with your tongue in her mouth or your fist in her cunt, is a psychological and emotional boundary. Depending on your feelings about yourself, your partner and sex, you may find penetration incredibly arousing or horribly invasive. Whatever you like or dislike and for whatever reason, you should always make yourself clear on the matter with partners, respecting their preferences too. If these don't accord with your own, discuss it. It's a strange fact, but many people seem to find it less intimidating or embarrassing to have sex with someone than to talk about sex with that same person! Perhaps a statement about how much more fearful it is to have our minds explored than our bodies? If you can't talk to a partner about sexual activities, and/or feel sexually frustrated or pressured as a result, perhaps you need to be discussing things other than just sex?

Sex Acts

Sado-masochism (SM)

Sado-masochism (usually referred to as SM) is primarily about the heightening of sexual excitement through pain.

This is the main thing which distinguishes it from sub/dom. Many people lump sado-masochism and sub/dom together into a general category, but this is not very helpful to our understanding of either, and the issue is further confused by the use of the terms top and bottom which can apply to both submissives and masochists, dominants and sadists. There are other crossovers too, as things like bondage and blindfolding or gagging can belong to both scenes. The term sadist is a very loaded one these days, and is rarely used in the SM scene as it carries connotations of abuse and non-consenting violence. Most of us in various aspects of our daily lives put ourselves through some kind of pain as an endurance, whether this is jogging, aerobics or merely staying at work or a club when we are tired. Most of the world's great physical triumphs such as conquering mountains or crossing oceans have been achieved by women and men prepared to suffer to prove something, while those around them may have stood wondering why anyone would want to do such a mad or potentially destructive thing. The emotional drives which some people express through climbing or white-water-rafting are very little different to those which inspire others to test their physical or emotional endurance under pain. How many of us have not wondered, while watching an old war film or reading about the heroines of the French Resistance, how well we would have stood up under torture, whether we would have told all? This curiosity about oneself is present in all of us, and for some women it's expressed through SM.

How we experience pain is affected by sexual arousal – the kind of pain experienced during an SM scene bears little relation to what a visit to the dentist might provide. During sexual excitement our tolerance of pain increases enormously, and at the point of orgasm it may barely be felt at all. Even women not interested or experienced in SM may well have enjoyed being bitten during sex, or having their nipples squeezed harder than usual. These sensations would be highly unpleasant and unacceptable outside the sex scene, but within it they add a charge of excitement. As with any form of sexual activity, there must be consent and good communication; with SM these must be stringently adhered to. You do not start beating someone who you know isn't into it, or 'not hear' their requests to have their hands untied because they're completely numb – this constitutes abuse. If that's what you're into you should probably seek professional advice for your problem.

If your scene is with your lover and you're experimenting, try writing down your fantasies independently, then comparing them. Any scene of this sort is about illusion and drama, and for it to really work the illusion must be sustained for the duration. SM is a powerful blend of trust, expectation, emotional bonding and heightened sexual awareness, which can range from tying-up and spanking to flogging, piercing and branding. Some women may prefer not to delve into their reasons for liking certain activites, but to understand your reasons and drives can be illuminating both within the scene itself and in your everyday life. What do you hope to feel or to get out of the situation? What do you hope to give and why?

There are a few rules to remember in practising bondage (or restraint as it's also called):

❖ Never leave someone tied up alone for more than a few minutes, particularly if they are gagged or blindfolded. You can pretend to leave them alone, but if you are a responsible top you'll never leave the bottom out of your sight for longer than the time it takes to use the bathroom. For some people, extensive restriction sessions such as 'mummification' involve being left alone in a meditative state while the top does something else: reads, cleans the house, talks to friends, but this is something that novices to SM should not consider as at requires considerable experience and trust.

❖ Always remember that thin materials like silk or nylon can tighten under stress and may be very hard to undo quickly, so consider keeping a pair of scissors handy.

❖ Avoid tying things around your partner's neck which may cut off her breathing. Some women enjoy simulated strangulation, but this should only really be done with the hands.

❖ There is the question of 'marking'. Is it OK to mark your partner? Does she enjoy being marked and if so, where is OK and where not? Even ropes and cuffs can mark. These are things that you may need to discuss before getting into a scene. Remember, some women mark more easily than others and the after-effects of your fun may last for weeks.

❖ Many people who enjoy SM practices use a 'safe word' code which may involve the top giving her bottom a special word to use when she has had enough of whatever is happening. Ideally this word should be something quite out of context, like 'lemons' or 'tarmac'. Words such as 'stop' or 'no' should be avoided as people often say, or even yell these things as a reflection of the experience, without meaning them literally. If the bottom is gagged then a signal can be agreed instead.

It is important to note here that many forms of SM activity – including consensual marking – are currently criminal offences in the United Kingdom (as evidenced by the 'Operation Spanner' cases). The choice is yours.

For many women, bondage is simply a part of fun or 'unusual' sex play. For those involved in SM, restriction is the first step in a wider scenario which may involve the use of pain.

Pain may be something as simple as dragging the fingernails down the partner's thighs or belly. It may involve slapping or spanking parts of the body, the buttocks, thighs, breasts or face – wherever feels most exciting. Biting the inner thighs, nipples, neck and vulva is particularly arousing for some women. For the top, feeling a partner's flesh between the teeth can be very exciting, and for the bottom, particularly if she is restrained, this can be an immense turn-on. Candle-wax is a popular means of delivering gentle pain – the hot wax can feel very intense for a few seconds, but then dissipates without leaving marks.

More serious SM games usually involve higher levels of pain. When SM is mentioned in this context it is probably flagellation – an umbrella term for any kind of beating, whipping or flogging – which first comes to mind. Beating can be done with any number of implements, most of them specialist, including whips, canes, paddles, quirts, straps and 'cats'. You can of course use the belt from round your waist (not the buckle end!). Whichever implement you use, remember it is the tip which leaves the most marks and causes the most pain.

The secret of successful flagellation is build-up; start slowly and carefully and work up to whatever your partner can take and wants. There can be something almost mesmerizing about beating someone who is used to and enjoys the pains and pleasures of being beaten, so tops need to beware of becoming so engrossed that they lose contact with the bottom and her reactions. Having your backside gently stroked when it has just been warmed up with a few strokes of a belt or cane can be very pleasurable, so it's a good idea to alternate the strokes with touching and feeling. Tops can try putting their fingers between their partner's legs and seeing iF she's excited by what's happening – after all that is the whole point of it.

If you are a novice and unsure of your aim, it's a good idea to practiSe on an inanimate object first; if you hit wildly you can injure your partner in an unnacceptable way. Never aim for the spine or kidney area as it's possible to damage these areas even with blows using the hand. If you are into having your breasts whipped, remember that blows to the breast tissue can cause lumps, and be very careful.

Many lesbians enjoy the use of clamps or clips which can be applied to the nipples, labia or any other part of the body fleshy enough to take them. These can be as tight as you can take, but should never be left on for more than 20 minutes, as after this time all circulation to the area will probably have stopped. The sensation from clamps can vary from a minor pressure or ache, to an intense and agonizing bite. Having clamped areas licked or sucked can be very exciting, for the bottom it may add to the stimulation and for the top the feeling of the metal or wood against her lips or tongue, juxtaposed with the softness of the clamped flesh, can be very arousing.

Having the clamp removed can be much more painful than wearing it, as the circulation and nerves respond again. Gentle massage can alleviate this. Because our breasts change during our cycle, what may feel good on nipples one week, may feel awful the next, so try keeping a selection of clamps with different pressures. Some women can take clamps directly on the clit, which for others would be impossible.

It's becomingly increasingly popular among some lesbians to have the vulva, nipples and navEl pierced. If the piercing is done with rings, these can be used as permanent sources of sexual stimulation as they can have weights hung from them; they can be linked together enhancing sensation and restricting movement. Try experimenting with what feels good where.

Unless you're lucky to have very understanding neighbours or no neighbours at all, don't forget about noise. Screams, yells and loud banging sounds can have people genuinely concerned for your safety; they may investigate themselves, or even call the police. If the latter arrive, remember much of what you're doing may be illegal.

A final note of caution. The more extreme end of SM is practised only by a small number of dedicated women. Activities which involve permanent marking – piercing during an SM scenario, branding, or heavy, extended flogging or kicking, are unlikely to be the sortS of things that the majority of women would enjoy. If you decide to experiment at this end of the spectrum, make sure it's with a woman or women that you trust absolutely, and that they are extremely experienced.

Sex Acts

Sex with men

For many lesbians the idea of sex with men, either in the present or the past, can be very unsettling. Because heterosexuality is still seen as the 'norm' in our culture, many lesbians and bisexual women constantly question their sexuality, in a way that most straight women simply never have to.

For many lesbians their sexuality means being woman-identified culturally, possibly preferring women as 'people', as friends. Some lesbians would argue that it is possible to be a lesbian and never have sex with a woman, that the identification is primarily emotional. If this is true, then it must also be possible to have sex with men and still be a lesbian. Yet another school of thought believes that it is the *act* which is homosexual or heterosexual, not the individual. This argument clears up 'minor' issues like bisexuality, self-identification and labelling, and simply states that any interaction with another woman is lesbian and any with a man is straight. *You* – the individual – are neither of these things, you are simply you!

For some lesbians, sex with a man is simply not part of their thinking. They've either done it and not been interested, or disliked it, or have never seen any reason to even consider it, being firmly focused on women since their first sexual awakenings. Not all women fall into these categories however, and for a seemingly increasing number of lesbians having sex with a man is something that does have a place in their lives, whether that is for procreative purposes, an expression of solidarity with gay men, pure cock lust, or simply fantasy. For many women who experience any or all of these feelings, having sex with a man could mean surrendering a cherished identity – one that has been carefully nurtured, often through difficult times. It isn't easy to surrender that,

and many women who do may then face the added burden of stigma from their peers and friends who feel they have 'let the side down' or 'let themselves down'.

The fact is that many lesbians fantasize about sex with men – whether they have ever experienced it in reality or not. They may feel awkward and uncomfortable about this, perhaps even fraudulent with their partners. Equally, many gay men fantasize and dream about sex with women, and up to 20 per cent of gay – as opposed to bisexual – identified men have sex with women in any given year. We all know that straight women fantasize about sex with other women and many explore this without ever thinking of themselves as lesbians – the same goes for straight men fantasizing about other men. Fifty per cent of *married* men report having had homosexual contact in their lifetime! Lesbians have fought very hard to be able to express our desires and passions for each other, let's not add to our own burden by persecuting ourselves for what we do, or wish to do, with less significant others.

If you are having sex with a man or men, or are considering doing so, then you will need to be aware of issues of HIV and safer sex to an even greater degree than you already are with your female partner(s). If your male partner is a sexually active gay man then you are placing yourself in a statistically much higher-risk category than you normally inhabit as a lesbian, and this is

something to be kept right to the front of your mind, however carried away you may get bouncing up and down on his cock. The simple rule is 'No sock, no cock!' Or as some safer sex posters put it: 'No glove, no love!' The risks of oral sex are still debated. Some cautious souls only have oral sex using a condom, others argue that this is preposterous. If you enjoy sucking cock, it's probably low risk without a condom as long as you don't let him come in your mouth. If you aren't familiar with how men come you may not know when this is likely to happen, so state in advance what you want and don't want just as you – hopefully – would with a woman. If you don't feel comfortable with it ,don't do it. If you are into fucking, either vaginally or anally, never even *begin* to do this without a condom.

If your partner is gay, perhaps it's a novel experience for him too, and it may be awkward for both of you. Just try and relax and if it happens it happens, if not you can always have a cuddle and a laugh about it afterwards. If your partner is a straight man and experienced, you may feel that he expects too much or is rushing you – just don't let it happen. If he isn't someone you can talk to openly you really shouldn't be there anyway. Although men and women are different anatomically and in a number of other important ways, ultimately the lesbian and straight sexual experiences have more similarities than differences and your expectations of and communication with a male partner should not be less than with a female, though they may be differently expressed and realized.

Many women find that their desires change with age or life circumstances. However we may like to think of it, for many people sexual desire is a changing and flexible phenomenon, affected by our past, our present and our future. As we get older and our past resolves itself, our focuses of desire may change. Women who have been heterosexual for fifty years may become attracted to women, and conversely lesbians may find themselves desiring men. We need to be open to the movements of our own feelings and changes. A gay closet is no more comfortable than a straight one when you come down to it and the door can be just as hard to push open. Standing between two cultures can be a hard and painful place to be, particularly if a sense of belonging is important to you. It can take great courage to stand there.

Submission & domination (sub/dom)

The sexual possibilities within power games have probably been acknowledged since humans began having sex. All cultures, across the world have taken slaves at some point in their histories and one of the purposes of this was sexual.

While many people may find the notion of sexual slavery politically incorrect or distasteful, the fact is that it has always been a part of the general sexual fantasies of both women and men. Over the last decade, perhaps as a response to issues around disease – HIV in particular – there has been an increasing interest in role-playing activities and power games. This interest has cut right across the spectrum of sexual identities, and many lesbians are now in the forefront of this exploration.

Many people, even those seriously involved in the 'scene', see sexual domination and submission – often called sub/dom – as an integral part of SM sex and although this is certainly true for some women, they can be two quite distinct forms of sexual enjoyment; not all submissives are masochists, nor are all masochists submissive. Relationships between women, as with any kind of relationship, can involve extensive role-playing and power games, on an everyday level. Some women enjoy taking this into their sexual life, perhaps extending their ordinary interactions or even reversing or swapping them. There has been considerable debate about this in feminist writing over the years, with feelings on both sides running very high. Some women feel that power-play is always damaging, some feel the opposite. We all need to make up our own minds about what we feel happy with. Each woman must choose her own routes to pleasure – and whether she is on top or not.

If you feel that sub/dom *is* something you would like to explore, either with your partner or with strangers, you may already have ideas or fantasies in your mind about what it's all about and, most importantly, which role you see yourself in. Perhaps it's both? You may even have a specific fantasy you would like to fulfil, or it may be a scene from a film you once saw. There are very many ways of setting up a sub/dom scene, but it might work best with a few rules established beforehand; for example how long the scene will last, how it will be brought to a close, what boundaries will exist. Some women may feel much safer experimenting with a partner or friend, while others might fear exposing themselves psychologically to someone who knows them well. Putting your sexual pleasure in the hands of someone you don't know can be exciting, but you may want to consider carefully whether you would really be prepared to take orders from a stranger, or let them restrain you or blindfold you. The degree of communication required in a scene is often greater than that in a straightforward sexual encounter, and this can be a good trust-building exercise between you and your partner.

One of the main components of any sub/dom scene has to be trust and of course, the consent of both parties in what can be an emotionally explosive situation. It is very easy to be tempted to abuse the game and use it, with a partner, to raise relationship issues in an inappropriate way; this is not part of the

scene and may end in real emotional violence or abuse. Unless you are entirely relaxed with the person you are playing with, it is probably best not to bother.

So what happens when you get into a scene? If it's your first time, or even if it's old stuff, you can – if it's good – expect to feel a wide range of conflicting emotions depending on which role you decide to adopt. If you choose to be submissive, or bottom, you may feel excited, humiliated, proud, frustrated, nervous and hopefully very, very turned on. All sorts of unacknowledged feelings around power relationships may surface. If you feel uncomfortable or nervous at any point it's important that you signal this in whatever way you and your partner have agreed (see Safe words). You can always take a break, have a drink and start again if you still want to.

If you are in the dominant, or top role, you may feel conflicting emotions too. You may experience feelings of power that are new to you and this can be both pleasurable and difficult at times. If you are a good dominant you will never forget that the power you have is a gift that can be withdrawn and if you are intelligent, you will remember that the role is simply that – a role – and not to be carried over into your relationship. There is a saying which goes roughly – 'to be a good top you need to have been a good bottom' – and there is a lot in this simple statement. Ideally you should never inflict on another person what

you have never experienced yourself, this is particularly true in SM where physical pain is part of the scenario. The beauty of having been submissive is that you have the double pleasure of commanding and knowing what it feels like to be commanded. If the scene is a good one it will, ideally, work to draw you and your 'submissive' closer together if she can express pleasure in, and gratitude for, your control and care of her, and you show similar feelings for her trust and compliance. Dominant roles may be particularly satisfying for women who are ordered about in their daily lives, something that most of us experience at one time or another.

Some women ask why anyone would want to be submissive. If you have a great deal of responsibility in your everyday life or career, it can be very soothing to have that responsibility lifted, even for a short time, to surrender thought and action to someone else. It may also be very exciting to play with the fantasy that you are so attractive to the dominant that they are prepared to take time and effort to have you in their control. The frustration that can arise from being forbidden to touch a partner or yourself while being driven crazy can be very exciting.

Role-playing can be particularly useful for women who feel ambivalent about their sexual drives, or who are shy about their sexual expression. If choice is removed and responsibility given up, it can be a very freeing experience to have to do something that you might not ordinarily choose or even like to do. You may come to find that you like a great many more things than you ever imagined – including losing control!

There are many aspects to sub-dom games which involve emotional risk, and humiliation is a part of this. Women who would loathe being humiliated in an ordinary context can derive great pleasure from being treated as a slave, an animal or even an inanimate object whose sole reason for existing during the scene is for the sexual pleasure of the top. Humiliation is, of course about emotional and mental pain, and for this reason many women find the idea of humiliation for sexual plea-sure disturbing, but for some women exploring fears and shame in a safe, sexual context can be helpful in dealing with the real thing. Some lesbians claim that enduring humiliation in an SM or sub/dom context allows them to face and overcome it in other situations. However, it's important to recog-nize that SM is not a substitute for psycholog-ical help, its single aim is simple – sexual

enjoyment for both parties. Like anything, humiliation can be practised for the 'wrong' reasons by either or both parties. If a bottom wishes to be humiliated for other than sexual reasons, or a top to humiliate out of spite or anger, then neither should really be involved in games of this sort.

Humiliation games can involve whatever your imagination and knowledge of your partner will stretch to. The top may interro-gate her partner about her sexual fantasies and either make a joke of them or tell her she's a slut and perhaps punish her physically for the thoughts; she may use insulting language or denigrate her, perhaps ask her what her friends or work colleagues would think, seeing her in such a position. Physical forms of humiliation can involve play with urine and faeces. Watersports (some people include enema play in this category), also called golden showers or golden rain, involve play with urine (piss); scat usually refers to playing with faeces (shit). The word scatology or 'scat' comes from the Greek *skatos* which refers not only to faeces and urine but to almost all bodily effluvia. Many women would probably be surprised to find themselves labelled as scatologists for kissing or licking their partner's tears, sucking her breast-milk or swallowing her saliva!

If you are interested in trying out games involving watersports or scat remember that they can be done in many contexts and for some people are not necessarily a part of humiliation activities, but simply belong to sex play. You can do as many things in a watersports or scat scene as your imagination will allow – try letting it roam back into your childhood! Because obedience in the area of bodily elimination is closely associated with early childhood, this type of play can be particularly interesting, being pissed on or pissing on someone can, for some women, require effort but be rewarding just because of the very tabooness of such activities. Whatever humiliation scenarios you come up with, it's important that both of you know that this is a game and when it's over, the everyday roles will be re-established intact. Tops may wish to be particularly loving and

attentive afterwards, a lot of trust has been given and received; celebrate that.

The truth of any situation involving consenting sub/dom is that the submissive is in control – always. She is the centre of attention, everything revolves around her, her actions, feelings and responses are what drives the situation. While being dominant can be enormously exciting and fulfilling, your gift to your partner is your imagination and skill in creating the scenario, it can also be exhausting and if your submissive is demanding or self-centred – and many submissives are! – unrewarding. On top can be a lonely place, so ensure that your play is mutual and fulfilling for both of you.

One of the greatest appeals of sub/dom is its theatricality, its potential for fun and challenge in either a new relationship or an established one. Find out from your partner, either directly or indirectly, what her fantasies in this area really are. Are they words, positions, clothing or bondage? It's not often we get to dress up as a Roman centurion or a harem girl *and* have fun sex!

Sex Acts

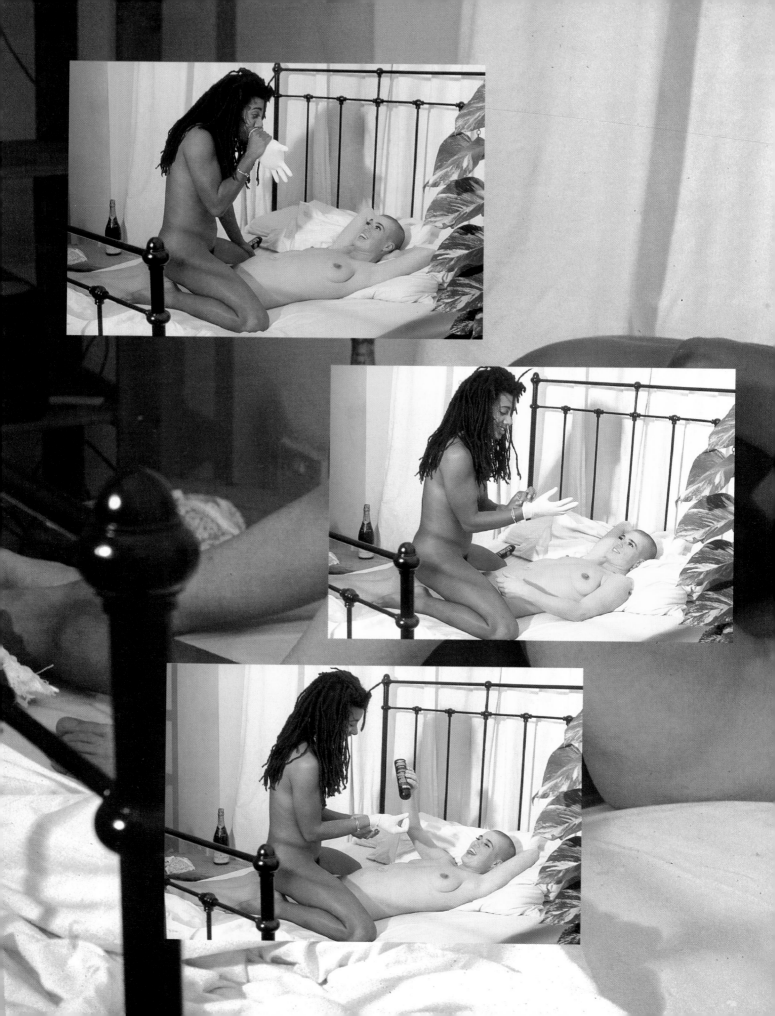

Tribadism

Also known as rubbing, humping and frottage, tribadism was once thought to be the main sexual activity of lesbians, and in the 19th century lesbians were often described as 'tribades'. It's a popular activity, though many women do it without knowing it has a name.

Tribadism is the technique of moving your vulva against that of your partner, or moving it over her thigh or buttocks or even breasts (nipple to vulva stimulation can be very exciting for some women, particularly if the nipples are erect). Women who prefer direct cunt to cunt contact use the scissor position which involves lying head to toe and 'fitting' together; holding wrists in this position creates extra contact and more variable body pressure.

This is also a good position for using a pliable, double-ended dildo or vibrator which can penetrate both partners at once – at this angle you have four openings to choose from! If your hands are free, stroke your partner or yourself; suck her toes or lick her feet.

Tribadism is a good way for women who like to move freely and vigorously to reach orgasm. Using lots of lube creates a great slippery sensation as you rub your vulva around your partner's body. If either of you are into real physicality or are feeling particularly athletic, try applying a silicone lube, edible oil, or lotion everywhere and have a wrestle before or as part of tribadism – a rubber sheet might be useful if you fancy making a real mess!

One of the best things about tribadism is that it can be done fully dressed; it is an anywhere-anytime activity, so why not play it to the full?!

Vanilla

Vanilla is not a sex act but rather an umbrella term for an attitude or approach to a variety of lesbian sex experiences. (It has other associations too: for some black women, sex with a white partner is called 'vanilla sex', referring only to 'colour' rather than the type of activities involved.)

Real vanilla is a plant related to the orchid family, its sweet and subtle spice was once considered an aphrodisiac. When used to describe the type of sex women have together, vanilla can be said lovingly by some women and disparagingly by others. For some lesbians, vanilla would mean tender, mutually caring sex, involving holding stroking, kissing, licking, sucking or rubbing parts of, or the entire, body. Direct sexual contact with a partner's genital area would probably include cunnilingus and finger-fucking.

For those women who use the word in a derogatory sense, it implies sex that is limited, boring or repetitive. It would probably not include the use of sex gear, any sort of fetishistic behaviour, any group activity, or any variant sex acts such as anal sex, rimming, or fisting.

As lesbians explore the further reaches of sexual experience, vanilla sex seems to be increasingly disparaged by some. But viewing either our own or others' behaviour in this way does little more than add stress to a world that is already stressful enough around attitudes to sex. So why bother? For many women, so-called vanilla sex remains at the central place of their sexual life with perhaps occasional trips into the unknown and 'dangerous'. For those who think of vanilla as boring – whatever extremes may be created, the comfort of a partner's arms and loving kiss are in fact probably just as vital.

index